7/ 2000

Women's Autobiographies, Culture, Feminism

American University Studies

Series XXVII
Feminist Studies

Vol. 6

PETER LANG
New York • Washington, D.C./Baltimore • Boston • Bern
Frankfurt am Main • Berlin • Brussels • Vienna • Canterbury

Kristi Siegel

Women's Autobiographies, Culture, Feminism

PETER LANG
New York • Washington, D.C./Baltimore • Boston • Bern
Frankfurt am Main • Berlin • Brussels • Vienna • Canterbury

Library of Congress Cataloging-in-Publication Data

Siegel, Kristi.
Women's autobiographies, culture, feminism / Kristi Siegel.
p. cm. — (American university studies XXVII: Feminist studies; vol. 6)
Includes bibliographical references and index.
1. Women's studies—Biographical methods. 2. Autobiography—
Women authors. 3. Mothers in literature. 4. Motherhood
in literature. I. Title. II. Series: American university
studies. Series XXVII, Feminist studies; vol. 6.
HQ1185.S54   305.4'092—dc21   98-50407
ISBN 0-8204-3678-X
ISSN 0042-5985

Die Deutsche Bibliothek-CIP-Einheitsaufnahme

Siegel, Kristi:
Women's autobiographies, culture, feminism / Kristi Siegel.
–New York; Washington, D.C./Baltimore; Boston; Bern;
Frankfurt am Main; Berlin; Brussels; Vienna; Canterbury: Lang.
(American university studies: Ser. 27,
Feminist studies; Vol. 6)
ISBN 0-8204-3678-X

Cover design by Lisa Dillon

The paper in this book meets the guidelines for permanence and durability
of the Committee on Production Guidelines for Book Longevity
of the Council of Library Resources.

Printed in the United States of America

To Ron, always

Acknowledgments

I have much to acknowledge and many people to thank. For their meticulous critiques and suggestions when this book was in its early stages, I would like to thank Professors Ihab Hassan, Gregory Jay, Cam Tatham, James Kuist, and Lynne Worsham of the University of Wisconsin-Milwaukee. On many occasions, Ihab Hassan's intellectual clarity steered me from blindness to insight. By encouraging me to take risks, Gregory Jay changed the entire focus of this book and, in the process, made it much richer than it would have been. More recently, I would like to thank various readers and mentors from Mount Mary College's English Department and, in particular, Ann Angel, Heidi Sjostrom, Sister Joan Cook, S.S.N.D., Florence Healy, and Jane Thompson. For her spiritual as well as intellectual impetus, I am especially grateful to Sister Luetta Wolf, S.S.N.D. Dr. Heidi Burns, my editor at Peter Lang Publishing, Inc., consistently offered direction, patience, encouragement, and wisdom. My gratitude to her is profound.

On a personal level, my debt to my husband, Ron, who invariably provided humor, perspective, and support, is immeasurable. Although this book's genesis is maternal, my gratitude to my mother and father remains equal. Finally I would like to thank my children, Aaron, Adam, Ross, and Elizabeth, who have patiently learned that "in a minute" generally meant several hours later.

Table of Contents

Preface

Although academic discourse is inherently more formal than personal, I have deliberately chosen to quote from many sources—both academic and non-academic. This medley of voices serves to illustrate the various ways the site of motherhood is textually erased or reduced to a metaphor in women's autobiographies, culture, and feminist theory. Further, I also quote women who have written from a mother's position, as it is precisely the maternal voice that has been silenced. Without these many maternal voices (including my own), this book would be perpetuating the very exclusion I critique. Like Adrienne Rich, I found writing "as a mother" both difficult and perilous. Yet, this book must be written from a mother's perspective. Too much has already been written *about* mothers. In Oedipal terms, Jocasta needs to speak for herself. After being censured for her mix of personal and academic material in *Of Woman Born*, Adrienne Rich wrote a cogent rebuttal:

> *Of Woman Born* was both praised and attacked for what was sometimes seen as its odd-fangled approach: personal testimony mingled with research, and theory which derived from both. But this approach never seemed odd to me in the writing. What still seems odd is the absentee author, the writer who lays down speculations, theories, facts, and fantasies without any personal grounding. (x)

In reality, academic writing often includes personal testimony. Theorists like Roland Barthes, Luce Irigaray, Ihab Hassan, Walter Benjamin, and others frequently provide personal references. More accurately, what may be at issue is the testimony's source. Fathers, sons, and daughters may "testify" while remaining safely within the intellectual/academic arena. Is a mother's testimony somehow *more* personal and *less* intellectual?

I

The Daughter's Discourse

The Site of Motherhood

The existence of an institution of motherhood, as opposed to an acknowledgment that there are simply mothers, is rarely questioned even though the proper qualities of motherhood are often the subject of debate. Motherhood is still largely treated as a given and as a self-evident fact rather than as the possible outcome of specific social processes that have a historical and cultural location which can be mapped.

—Carol Smart "Deconstructing Motherhood"

This book focuses on women's autobiographies, culture, and feminism to examine how mothers have been represented by their daughters as well as by themselves. In analyzing how a mother's self and often body become textually configured a larger question is also being asked. What is the site of motherhood? Or, to word this question more specifically, as Dana Heller does in her work, *Family Plots: The De-Oedipalization of Popular Culture* (1995), has the position of motherhood been adequately critiqued? Feminists themselves often seem at a loss to describe the work and value of a mother. Heller contends that "it remains the task of an emergent feminist social critique to address the ambivalence toward the Oedipal mother" (76). This work, in part, proposes to begin that critique by examining a mother's role in modern society and considering how motherhood remains an uneasy site both in text and culture.

While the recent debates on the state of the American family and their values appear to treat all members of a family, often the question really being asked concerns only one member: "What is a mother's proper role?" Certainly women's roles have become more diverse in the past few decades; more women than not now combine careers and motherhood. While women "have come a long way" in terms of their cultural value, it may be the very diversity of contemporary women's roles that creates their "value." How valued, even yet, is the actual work of a mother? To use the classic Oedipal configuration, does a mother still lack power (in Freud's terms) and the access to language (in Lacan's terms)? Dana Heller's study, referred to above, depicts the difficulty inherent in any sort of static definition of "family" but sees, despite the trend toward de-Oedipalization in modern culture, the pervasiveness of the "family romance" outlined by Freud. Heller sums up Freud's analysis of the mother's role in the family romance as one that remains ambivalent—only the mother can know the "secret of paternity"—and devalued since Oedipal dynamics work to silence the mother. In Freudian configuration, since the mother cannot access the symbolic order and phallic power, this site of power and language belongs to the father alone who thus occupies "the privileged site of origin and social meaning, while it constructs the mother as a voiceless and potentially deceptive enclosed space where mysteries of multiple voice are encoded in a language no one can read" (Heller paraphrasing Freud 32–3). In this analysis the mother's language emerges as irrational babble, her maternity arouses distrust, and her work remains outside of the public/cultural—and therefore valued—sphere. To construct the question in dangerously general terms—motherhood's various social and ethnic experiences cannot be conflated—does modern culture now value motherhood and the work of mothering? Heller sees our attitude toward mothers as one still riddled with ambivalence, a combination of "maternal idealization and contempt" (76).

While in no way serving as a model for all maternal experience, an episode from the relatively recent television series *thirtysomething* effectively dramatizes many of the conflicts surrounding contemporary motherhood. Briefly, the show deals with the problems of a young, white, middle-class (yuppie) family, Hope and Michael Steadman, their infant daughter, Jane (Janie), along with their extended family of "thirtysomething" friends. In the show's eighth episode, entitled "Weaning," which aired on December 8, 1987, Janie's decreasing dependency on her mother—due to the weaning process—prompts Hope to question what she should be doing with her life. Prior to having a child, Hope was an ambitious and talented researcher/writer of consumer protection articles. Up until the time of weaning, Hope has been relatively content and sees nursing Janie as a measurable value, a relationship between producer and consumer. Hope's sense that she cannot supply her daughter with something of value without the tangible flow of milk re-plays the workplace's dynamics. For whatever reasons, Hope herself has a difficult time assigning value to mother's work. If her daughter can become more independent, Hope concludes she must make similar strides. Hope's insecurity escalates when she goes out to dinner with Michael and some of his business associates. During dinner, Hope repeatedly tries to interject comments but no one is hearing her. Hope's status as a mother effectively encodes her language as irrational babble; the others see her as a *mother*: as a body rather than an intellect. As the conversation ensues Hope's inability to connect with the others is underscored by having her voice emerge as slow and out of sync, the way a voice sounds on a phonograph when it's played at the wrong speed. The only time Hope does get a question directly addressed to her occurs when they are discussing how to market diapers and turn to Hope for her maternal expertise. Hope, startled by finally being recognized, reacts by over-reacting and launches into a long, verbose diatribe on chemicals and consumerism. Although Hope has framed her words intellectually, her attempt to use phallic discourse fails. They stare at her with incomprehension, interpret her speech as babble, and turn away from her again.

Not surprisingly, Hope soon decides she must re-enter the public sphere by resuming her career. While Hope ponders whether to go back to work (and even after she's begun working), the frequent scene-cuts to Hope tenderly holding Janie or Hope looking sadly at the young mother surrogate she hires to care for Janie, make the episode's outcome clear. Since it's apparent early on that Hope will choose to stay at home instead of pursuing her career (as if this were a simple either/or choice), it is very interesting to see how—in our politically correct culture—they will have Hope make this decision without her seeming to be oppressed by patriarchy. Obviously, Michael's role requires careful treatment. To highlight *thirtysomething*'s distance from sitcoms like *Father Knows Best* or *Leave It to Beaver* where the law of the father prevails, Michael offers unflagging good will and support for whatever decisions Hope makes. Importantly, Hope's realization that her career proves detrimental to her family must come from sources other than the show's "father." Accordingly, Hope's decision emerges from her interaction with other women, not other men. Hope's job takes place at a business where there are only women. Hope sees herself in a younger woman working there who is childless and utterly goal-oriented. Hope feels threatened by the younger woman—who has far more time and energy than Hope—but also sees— just as she is scripted to see—the emptiness of the woman's life. Hope's attempts to write at home fail; Janie interrupts her, the house becomes a shambles, and Michael (the breadwinner) begins to lose sleep as he tries to support Hope in her career. Further, Hope's babysitter mentions some minor feat Janie accomplished during the day and Hope feels she's missed a milestone. When Hope, exhausted, finally turns in the report, her boss, a strong African-American woman, gives it to her straight and tells Hope that while the work was good it was far from her best. The three women, like the Spirits of Christmas Past, Present, and Future that haunt Scrooge, serve as caveats; Hope sees that an outside career plus motherhood jeopardizes her entire family. By having Hope's decision enabled exclusively by women, *thirtysomething* appears progressive while reinscribing traditional family roles. Whether Hope's choice is right or wrong remains both unanswerable and irrelevant. The fact that Hope has a choice at all immediately differentiates her from most mothers. What is more important is the show's outcome and how that outcome has come about. Ostensibly, Hope has received no pressure from Michael either to stay at home or go back to work. Hope's final decision appears to derive entirely from her own conclusions and her interactions with other women. Paradoxically, however much the producers/writers of *thirtysomething* desire to display their political correctness, the show's conclusion nevertheless re-enacts the unspoken core of the current family values debates. Mothers should stay at home.

The image of mother at home, tending to the needs of her family, so popularized by sitcoms in the 1950s and 1960s, is actually a cultural anomaly. As Shari L. Thurer points out in *The Myths of Motherhood: How Culture Reinvents the Good Mother* (1994) the "fifties were an aberration" (250). Rather than being the norm, the nuclear family depicted by television families such as the Cleavers, the Nelsons, the Reeds *et al*, reflect a family model that existed for a very short time (the 1950s and early 1960s) in Western culture. Thurer's point is not to disparage or laud the nuclear family but merely to point out that the frozen image of mom at home caring for her family while dad goes out to make money does not accurately reflect our history. As Thurer explains, a mother's role and what culture perceives as the ideal mother, has undergone many permutations over time. More importantly, what we view as some sort innate ideal model of motherhood is always a social construct, an invention rather than a given.

Despite the relative brevity of the "at-home mom" in American society, that image remains our enduring model of motherhood. While viewing the at-home mother as the "ideal," the mother's dominance on the homefront was simultaneously the focus of criticism. As Thurer points out, in both literary and critical texts, mothers were blamed for society's ills. For mothers, it was a classic lose-lose situation. Mothers who did not stay at home were viewed as unnatural (and caused their family psychic harm) while mothers who did remain at home were also blamed for every neurotic/psychotic impulse their family later evinced. Oddly, even many feminists participated in the collective mother-bashing and provided accounts of how they were "victimized" by their mothers (270). Thurer, citing the arguments of Nancy Chodorow and Susan Contratto, speculates that the reason many feminists exclude mothers from their celebration of women hinges on their tendency to see mothers

as all-powerful and thus all-responsible: "the cause of feminists' de-
bunking of mom [is their] belief—to everyone's belief—in an all-powerful mother, who, because she is fully responsible for how her children
turn out, is blamed for everything, from her child's limitations to the cri-
ses of human existence" (270).

Persistently, motherhood remains a site of ambivalence. The power
mothers are imagined to have—in the domestic arena—is often viewed
as destructive. Outside of the home, in the cultural/intellectual sphere,
mothers have/had no power at all. As Thurer astutely notes, by the late
1970s "it was still only Portnoy's complaint that mattered, not his
mother's" (286). Further, if mothers were complaining it was not in
print; the autobiographies and books that were being written emerged
from their daughters.

Since traditional autobiographies highlight a person's spiritual and
cultural course, women—who are socially constructed as bodies—have
to work doubly hard to be "worthy" autobiographical subjects. If women
in general are perceived as bodies, the perception escalates for mothers
for, Shirley Neuman has noted, the "figure of the mother is determined
by her body more intensely than the figure of woman" ("Autobiography"
12). Not surprisingly daughters as autobiographers quickly realize they
need to represent their mothers and their relationship to their mothers
very carefully. A savvy daughter intuits that too close an identification
with her mother puts her own cultural value at risk.   Similarly, when
Hope (from *thirtysomething*), spoke from the mother's position her
speech was perceived as irrational babble; to be heard she needed to
speak from the daughter's position, a position culturally received as less
embodied and more intellectual. To be recognized as worthy autobiographical subjects, then, daughters must adopt many of the conventions
inherent in classical autobiography. The assumptions of traditional autobiography mime many of the beliefs embedded in Western culture: e.g.,
the centrality of white males, the privileging of mind over body, the importance of the public versus private sphere, and so forth. Consequently,
the way in which daughters often efface or distort their mothers'

representations to conform to autobiography's expectations re-plays the dynamics of dominant culture. By using a primarily feminist psychoanalytic approach to analyze the textual gyrations both daughters (and mothers) manifest when they write about their mothers (or write from the mother's position) larger questions may be broached. What is the role of motherhood? What is the value of motherhood in Western culture? In looking at how the image of motherhood "plays out" in women's autobiographies, I also posit how mothers are represented and configured in a larger cultural arena. Further, to parallel as closely as possible dominant cultural beliefs, my study focuses on women's autobiographies that were written for publication and follow—for the most part—the genre's traditional conventions.

Situating Women's Autobiography

> Matrophobia can be seen as a womanly splitting of the self, in the desire to become purged once and for all of our mothers' bondage, to become individuated and free. The mother stands for the victim in ourselves, the unfree woman, the martyr. Our personalities seem dangerously to blur and overlap with our mothers; and, in a desperate attempt to know where mother ends and daughter begins, we perform radical surgery.
>
> —Adrienne Rich, *Of Woman Born*

Oscar Wilde, in *The Importance of Being Earnest*, writes that "All women become like their mothers. That is their tragedy" (363). Wilde's comment contains a number of assumptions. Wilde sees women in a state of binary opposition: we may be daughters or mothers. Within this binary opposition, the position of mother carries a negative charge. According to Wilde, all women, whether they actually become mothers, will become *like* their mother and this is their tragedy. Wilde's comment, though hyperbolic and sardonic, is, from a cultural standpoint, partially true.

Within the context of Wilde's play, we may make some speculations about the nature of the "tragic" transformation from daughter to
mother. First the mother is older, therefore less desirable and less valu-
able as a commodity. If, as Luce Irigaray asserts, the "woman exists
only as an occasion for mediation, transaction, transition, transference
between man and his fellow man" (193), the mother, whose transference
has already been enacted, is absent from the marketplace. Further, in
raising and guiding her children, the mother becomes a figure of power, a
veritable "Gorgon" (363), as a character in Wilde's play puts it, as her
authority is in direct opposition to the passivity he associates with the
daughter's charms. Looked at closely, we may see, however, that the
mother's power is relegated to the private sphere. Typically, the
mother's authority does not extend beyond home and family.

For the daughter, then, the mother becomes a figure simultaneously
powerful and impotent. While the mother may reign supreme in the
kingdom of childhood, historically, the daughter soon learns that the father is more dominant in the public sphere. Sons, of course, learn this as
well but their relationship to their mothers logically ends in separation.
Conversely, for the daughter the mother functions as a distant mirror; the
daughter, early on, constructs herself around the figure of the mother and
sees the mother as the projection of her own future.

Many female theorists have written about the importance of the
mother-daughter relationship. A short list of influential texts include
Adrienne Rich's *Of Woman Born: Motherhood as Experience and Insti-
tution* (1976), Dorothy Dinnerstein's *The Mermaid and the Minotaur:
Sexual Arrangements and Human Malaise* (1977), Nancy Chodorow's
*The Reproduction of Mothering: Psychoanalysis and the Sociology of
Gender* (1978), Carol Gilligan's *In a Different Voice: Psychological
Theory and Women's Development* (1982), Jane Gallop's *The Daugh-
ter's Seduction: Feminism and Psychoanalysis* (1982*)*, Nancy K. Miller's
The Poetics of Gender (1986), Jessica Benjamin's *The Bonds of Love:
Psychoanalysis, Feminism, and the Problem of Domination* (1988),
Carolyn Heilbrun's *Writing a Woman's Life* (1988), Marianne Hirsch's

The Mother-Daughter Plot: Narrative, Psychoanalysis, Feminism (1989), Laurie Corbin's *The Mother Mirror: Self-Representation and the Mother-Daughter Relation in Colette, Simone de Beauvoir, and Marguerite Duras* (1996), and various essays by Shirley Neuman and Jane Flax. Briefly, I would like to focus on the theorizations of Nancy Chodorow, Adrienne Rich, and Marianne Hirsch. In Chodorow's formulation the bond daughters form with their mothers during the pre-Oedipal period make girls "experience themselves as less separate than boys, as having more permeable ego boundaries" (93). Because of a girl's (versus a boy's) more connected relationship to her mother, Chodorow posits that girls are more empathetic and focused on the feelings of others (167). Importantly, Chodorow's depiction of women as other-oriented becomes a dominant theme in theorizations about women's autobiography. As adults, Chodorow explains how daughters who have been mothered reproduce motherhood to recapture the "sense of dual unity they had with their mother" (200). While Adrienne Rich also foregrounds the closeness of the mother-daughter relationship (and, like Chodorow, locates its genesis pre-Oedipally) Rich's study shows more anger: both at the matrophobia feminists (and Rich herself) often evince and at the institutions of patriarchy that she feels have diluted and distorted the mother-daughter bond. Marianne Hirsch would concur with Rich's assessment of the mother-daughter narrative as "the great unwritten story" (225). While Hirsch believes this story is starting to be written, too often the mother still remains excluded from the "family romance": "so long as the figure of the mother is excluded from theory *psychoanalytic feminism* cannot become a *feminist psychoanalysis*" (12). Like Rich, Hirsch also identifies our society's matrophobia and the tendency—even among feminists—to be unable to really hear their mothers' stories (28). Even yet, Hirsch asserts, feminists opt to write from a "daughterly" perspective and thus "collude with patriarchy in placing mothers into the position of object" (163). What emerges here, particularly in the theories of Rich and Hirsch, is the ambivalence daughters feel towards their mothers. Instinctively, daughters recognize their mothers' culturally devalued status and have fled from the domestic prison-house in which they see their mothers ensnared. As Laurie Corbin also notes, mothers might function as "mirrors" for their daughters, but it is often an unwelcome reflection (120).

For the daughter as autobiographer this presents a dilemma. To write the traditional autobiography—a work intended for publication—versus diaries, journals, and other private or "found" documents, presumes entry into the public sphere. Up until recently and perhaps even yet, this meant that a woman needed to act like a man. Georges Gusdorf's well-known discussion of autobiography is not only pronominally gendered but also presumes a person certain of "his" worth and centrality: "The man who takes delight in thus drawing his own image believes himself worthy of a special interest. Each of us tends to think of himself as the center of a living space: I count, my existence is significant to the world, and my death will leave the world incomplete" (29). To say, then—in Lacanian terms—that autobiography has traditionally been a phallic discourse renders symbolic what is in fact real: the most famous—or at least most critiqued—autobiographies have been written by famous men (e.g., St. Augustine, Jean-Jacques Rousseau, Benjamin Franklin, Henry Adams, Henry James, Jean-Paul Sartre, etc.); its form has been shaped by men's lives and as a genre it has largely been defined by male theorists. What is imaginary or symbolic (in a Lacanian sense) about that? As Jane Gallop trenchantly points out, the separation of the phallus from the penis has some distinct advantages. Obviously it is easier for a man to speak of the symbolic nature of the phallus than it is for a woman since she literally does not have a penis and consequently does not possess phallic power:

> The question of whether one can separate 'phallus' from 'penis' rejoins the question of whether one can separate psychoanalysis from politics. The penis is what men have and women do not . . . . But as long as the attribute of power is a phallus which refers to and can be confused (in the imaginary register?) with a penis, this confusion will

support a structure in which it seems reasonable that men have power and women do not. And as long as psychoanalysts maintain the separability of 'phallus' from 'penis,' they can hold on to their 'phallus' in the belief that their discourse has no relation to sexual inequality, no relations to politics. (97)

And the politics of autobiography *is* that it has largely been a genre written by, controlled by, and defined by men.

Tracing Women's Autobiographical Theory

One gathers from this enormous modern literature of confession and self-analysis that to write a work of genius is almost always a feat of prodigious difficulty . . . . But for women, I thought, looking at the empty shelves, these difficulties were infinitely more formidable. In the first place, to have a room of her own, let alone a quiet room or a sound-proof room, was out of the question, unless her parents were exceptionally rich.

—Virginia Woolf, *A Room of One's Own*

The central position of men in autobiographical discourse may be demonstrated merely by looking at recent history. Although women have certainly been producing autobiographies and despite the fact that autobiographical theory has rapidly escalated in the past twenty years, far less has been written—exclusively—about women's autobiography. Further, nearly everything that has been written has been written by women. Most of the women note the dearth of scholarship on women's autobiographies. Domna Stanton, in "Autogynography: Is the Subject Different?" describes how her 1983 search for secondary materials on female autobiographies yielded only one listing in the card catalogue: *Women's Autobiography: Essays in Criticism*, edited by Estelle Jelinek.

Stanton's reading of Jelinek's preface corroborated the apparent absence of secondary material. In the preface, Jelinek refers to her experience writing her dissertation in 1976, when she was able to find "practically no criticism on women's autobiographies, except for that on Gertrude Stein's" (ix). Her dismay with the lack of secondary materials led her to compile the 1980 collection of essays in order "to encourage such criticism" (ix).

Norrine Voss, in "'Saying the Unsayable': An Introduction to Women's Autobiography," (1986) finds little improvement, asserting that in "no other literary genre as in autobiography have women produced such a varied and rich canon, yet received so little recognition for their achievements" and that a perusal of "books about American autobiography might lead one to conclude that Gertrude Stein was the only American woman to write an autobiography" (218). My own preliminary search in 1988 for works of theory and criticism on women's autobiography uncovered only fourteen separate references. Few of the fourteen dealt primarily with autobiographical theory and only four were book-length studies.

Many women writing on women's autobiography trace the major male arguments and refer in a paragraph or less to the work on autobiography that has been done by women. Inadequately discussing what has been written about women's autobiography only perpetuates erasure. Further, since I offer an alternative principle for discussing women's autobiography—I argue that women's autobiography is distinguished by its uneasy relationship to the body and maternity—it is first helpful to discuss the existing methods and models of women's autobiographical criticism.

Norrine Voss's categorization of the scholarship on women's autobiography provides a convenient way to organize the existing studies. Voss sees the theorists (of women's autobiography) taking three main approaches:

- archeological studies;
- studies of groups of autobiographies possessing a common trait; and

- studies centering on the subject of "difference," that is, on how women's autobiographies differ from men's.

In light of the past few years, another category could be added to Voss's list:

- studies emphasizing the difference among women themselves, i.e., studies emphasizing the ethnic, cultural, and sexual differences that reconfigure generalized formulations about women's autobiography.

The first approach—the archeological "dig" method—though in progress—has a long way to go. At the University of Wisconsin-Milwaukee library, for example, the majority of American women's autobiographies published during or before the nineteenth century, such as those of Susanna Rowson, Caroline Gilman, Elizabeth Stuart Phelps, Lydia Louise Ann Very, Harriet Prescott Spoffard, Jane Marsh Parker, and others, are available only on microfilm. The difficulties of reading and/or copying an entire book from microfilm nearly erases these texts from consideration. The necessity of doing just that type of tedious work, however, may be inferred from Stanton's frustration in trying to write intelligently on women's autobiography "when the primary and secondary sources were only beginning to emerge" (9).

The second method of inquiry examines groups of autobiographies sharing a common feature such as race, religion, occupation, or subject. The pitfall that may occur with this mode of inquiry is the tendency to use a small sampling to make large claims. Elizabeth Winston, in "The Autobiographer and her Readers: From Apology to Affirmation," serves as a case in point. Winston's selected group consists of a "sample of fourteen autobiographies of professional women writers, published between 1852 and 1965" (94). From this sampling, Winston concludes that women autobiographers "whose autobiographies were published after 1920 . . . no longer apologized for their careers and successes" (93). This sweeping statement, precisely dated no less, recalls the more tongue-in-cheek proclamation of Virginia Woolf regarding the advent of modernism: "On or about December 1910 human nature changed . . . . All human relations shifted" (qtd. in Bradbury 33).   And even within Winston's small sampling there are exceptions.   Harriet Martineau, whose autobiography places her in the chronological middle of the 1850 to 1920 group, presents a problem in her "untimely" assertiveness. Winston adroitly handles this apparent deviation from her thesis by re-categorizing Martineau as a "transitional figure, somewhat ahead of her time" (94).   In my reading, the critics who successfully used the "selected group" approach limited their observations to their discussed group and paid attention to the erasure of race, culture, history, and ethnicity, that may take place by making any small group representational.

The area of women's autobiographical theory I would like to address particularly, however, centers on the question of "difference." The third and most prevalent approach women scholars have used in discussing autobiography is to determine what differences exist between men's and women's autobiographies. Certainly, a woman's orientation to traditional autobiography is different from a man's. A man—a son—may safely identify with his father in his autobiography since it is likely his father occupies a public, and thus valued, position. On the other hand, since an autobiography highlights a subject's passage into the public or male sphere, the daughter must consider carefully how she will represent her relationship with her mother. A woman could, of course, model her autobiography after her father but she would still need to confront her relationship to her mother. Though many contemporary mothers now operate in the public sphere the majority of women's autobiographies are written from the daughter's perspective and these daughters have mothers who, for the most part, had not entered the public sphere.

Consequently, though a daughter as a child may imitate her mother, she cannot, in writing an autobiography, very well demonstrate her public value by having her mother—a figure traditionally typifying private, disempowered space—serve as her model. The point is not that autobiography disrupts an otherwise untroubled and symbiotic relationship between mother and daughter but that autobiography takes an already ambivalent relationship and encourages its erasure, textual flattening, and distortion. Sidonie Smith, similarly commenting on this dilemma, explains that as the daughter "appropriates the story and speaking posture of the representative man, she silences that part of herself that identifies her as a daughter of her mother. Repressing the mother in her, she turns away from all that is domesticated and disempowered culturally and erases the trace of sexual difference and desire" ("Poetics" 53). What I would argue is that women's autobiography, and it *is* primarily the daughter's discourse, is characterized by its inability to silence the maternal. Rather than being erased, the daughter's representation of the mother becomes instead a charged space—a textual abyss—in women's autobiographies.

The theorization on "difference" that has been done in the past twenty-five years treats both style and content. Patricia Meyer Spacks is one of the first to articulate a theory of difference in women's autobiography. In her 1973 article, "Reflecting Women," she states that in "autobiographies by indirection, journals and collections of letters, women project a sense of themselves and of their writing's purpose sharply opposed to that of men" (26). In her article, however, Spacks does not clearly define how she sees women's autobiographies as differing from those by men. One problem may be in the comparison of women's journals and diaries—automatically "non"-traditional autobiographies—to the male autobiographies clearly falling within generic definitions.

What difference Spacks identifies concerns the opposing ways men and women react to "limitations," i.e., "the struggle of men, their autobiographies suggest, is to surmount limitations; the struggle of women, often, to circumvent them, to operate so smoothly within limits that they seems to have no hampering effect" (27). Spacks theorizes that one of the ways women circumvent their limitations is to write about them: "to transform difficult reality into glamorous myth" (27). The woman's mode of circumvention leads Spacks' to theorize an inner/outer dichotomy between female/male autobiography:

> "Man's attention is primarily directed outward, and woman's inward," writes Helene Deutsch in *Psychology of Women*. In their memoirs and journals, women use the knowledge and tradition gained from the outer world as a way of shaping and comprehending their inner experience; this operation partly accounts for the "mythic" aspect of their self-presentation. (27)

In her 1977 article, "Women's Stories, Women's Selves," Spacks sees women orienting the subject of their autobiographies around the ideology of "goodness" and "selflessness" society has imposed upon them. Generally, the voices of women show a "stress on service, love, weakness, inadequacy, and fear" while men "write most typically of the struggle for power and mastery . . ." (36). Women, Spacks posits, opt for a personal world based on "practice" rather than the more theoretical world devised by male culture:

> "Culture" is a male concept. The woman dismisses talk about it as mere "babble," her own orientation personal. Its personal quality, however, implies her capacity—contradicting Freud's generalization—to accept "the great exigencies of life" not by explaining them (as men do with their "babble") but by enduring them . . . (46)

Estelle Jelinek, in her 1976 paper, "Discontinuity and Order: A Comparison of Women's and Men's Autobiographies" as well as in the 1980 book she edits, *Women's Autobiography: Essays in Criticism*, emerges as another pioneer in this debate. Jelinek sees women's autobiographies manifesting a narrative style that is "disconnected, fragmentary, or organized into self-sustained units rather than connecting chapters" (17) and treating, as their focus, "their personal lives" (8). Men, conversely, emphasize the "public aspects of their lives" (7) and use a "chronological, linear narrative" since men are "socially conditioned to pursue the single goal of a successful career" (17).

Jelinek's position remains unchanged in her 1986 book, *The Tradition of Women's Autobiography: From Antiquity to Present*. There she restates her position (first formulated in her 1976 dissertation) that the "emphasis [in women's autobiographies] remains on personal matters" rather than the "professional, philosophical, or historical events that are more often the subject of men's autobiographies" (xiii). The narrative dichotomy in women's life stories also persists: "the style of these autobiographies is, for the most part, also similar, and it is integral with such a paradoxical self-image: episodic and anecdotal, nonchronological and disjunctive" (xiii). Though Jelinek now notes exceptions to the male/female categorization she feels these autobiographers are writing in opposition to their gender: "Although there are a fair number of exceptions—women writing in typically male progressive and linear narratives and men writing anecdotally and disjunctively, especially in recent decades—the pattern does persist" (xiii).

Jelinek's observation also becomes a common citation in the works of other women theorists. Suzanne Juhasz, writing in 1978, cites Jelinek's work in her article, " 'Some Deep Old Desk or Capacious Hold-All': Form and Women's Autobiography." Juhasz, who is speculating primarily on unpublished autobiographies done by students in her class, proposes to explore "autobiographical form and its relation to the shape of women's lives" (663). Juhasz sees a deep relationship to the "diary form [often excluded from studies of autobiography] and women's lives" (664). Juhasz, like Jelinek and Spacks, describes the fragmentation, and the personal/practical rather than the public/theoretical orientation in women's lives:

> Women's work, whether it be as manager of houses or households, shows less a pattern of logical and linear development towards some clear goal than one of repetitive, cumulative, cyclical content and hence meaning. Women, especially because they are so involved

with interpersonal relationships, 'have a more complex, interdepend-
ent relationship with the world than men do . . . women are concerned
with the context, while men are forever trying to ignore it for the sake
of something they can abstract from it,' as the psychologist David
McClelland writes. (664)

The diary, then, would seem to be a form custom-made to fit the
"shape of women's lives." In support, Juhasz quotes Jelinek: "As Estelle
C. Jelinek points out in her comparative study of 'autobiographies
proper' by women and men, irregularity rather than orderliness has in-
formed many literary self-portraits by women" (665).

In 1980, Lynn Z. Bloom and Orlee Holder ("Anais Nin's *Diary* in
Context") also treat the male/female codification and directly reference
Juhasz and Jelinek, stating that men's autobiographies are "structured,
orderly. In contrast, as Suzanne Juhasz and Estelle Jelinek have observed, women's autobiographies tend to be much less clearly organized,
much less synthetic . . ." (207).

In 1980, Juhasz again expresses the suitability of the diary form as a
literary paradigm for the shape of women's lives ("Towards a Theory of
Form in Feminist Autobiography: Kate Millett's *Flying* and *Sita*; Maxine
Hong Kingston's *The Woman Warrior*"). Juhasz observes that a woman
telling a story will omit no detail, "because all details have to do with her
sense of the nature of 'what happened'" while a man will "give you the
gist, the result, the *point* of the event" (223). Women's lives, Juhasz asserts, tend to have a form "like the stories that they tell" and she proceeds
to depict what women's lives are like: "they show less a pattern of linear
development toward some clear goal than one of repetitive, cumulative,
cyclical structure . . . . Dailiness matters to most women; and dailiness is
by definition never a conclusion, always a process" (223–24).

Juhasz, here, may assume too much. I am not sure, for instance,
whether many men do not also consider their lives "repetitive, cumulative" and "cyclical," i.e., a daily grind. Nor am I sure how much "daili-

ness matters to most women" and if, in fact, this preoccupation permeates their writing style.

Mary G. Mason, in "Other Voices: Autobiographies of Women Writers" (1980), although she does not cite Jelinek, Spacks, or Juhasz, similarly comments on the "mode of interior disclosure" (209) in women's autobiographies and states that "the egoistic secular archetype that Rousseau handed down to his Romantic brethren in his *Confessions*, shifting the dramatic presentation to an unfolding self-discovery where the characters and events are little more than aspects of the author's evolving consciousness, finds no echo in women's writing about their lives" (210). I think, though I largely agree with Mason's conclusion, that she might find an "echo" of the male "egoistic secular archetype" in the autobiographies of Gertrude Stein.

In Judith Kegan Gardiner's article, "On Female Identity and Writing About Women" (1982), the characteristics of women and men are again limned:

> Female identity is a process, and primary identity for women is more flexible and relational than for men. Female gender identity is more stable than male gender identity. Female infantile identifications are less predictable than male ones. Female social roles are more rigid and less varied than men's. (184)

Gardiner stresses the "fluid and flexible aspects" of women's lives and connects this with the observation that "women's writing often does not conform to the generic prescriptions of the male canon" (185). In support, Gardiner states "Recent scholars conclude that autobiographies by women tend to be less linear, unified, and chronological than men's autobiographies" (185).

In brief, theorists such as Jelinek, Spacks, Bloom, Juhasz, Gardiner, and others articulate a male/female binary: women's autobiographies, they posit, are stylistically disconnected and fragmented while the content is characteristically personal in focus. Men's autobiographies, on the other hand, have a linear, seamless style and in content present their public lives. While the theorization of "difference" in women's autobiographies is an ongoing debate, the recurring binary codification of gender outlined above raises several issues.

What, for example, would constitute an adequate sampling to demonstrate consistent differences in style and content between men and women's autobiographies? Exceptions to the binary theorization immediately come to mind. Jean-Jacques Rousseau's autobiography, the *Confessions*, paves the way for personal revelation, while Edith Wharton's autobiography, *A Backward Glance*, is chilly in its reticence. The autobiographies of Roland Barthes (*Barthes on Barthes*), Michel Leiris (*Manhood*), Ihab Hassan (*Out of Egypt*), or Vladimir Nabokov (*Speak, Memory*) demonstrate temporal disjuncture and fluidity of style while the autobiographies of Ellen Glasgow (*The Woman Within*), Charlotte Perkins Gilman (*The Living of Charlotte Perkins Gilman*), and Eudora Welty (*One Writer's Beginnings*) proceed linearly, use a straightforward style, and—in large measure—do treat their careers, their so-called public lives.

If, as Michel Foucault has argued, our bodies are culturally inscribed by imaginary margins, how precisely may we differentiate public from private experience? What constitutes a woman's public experience? In broad terms, what is *private* is hidden or concealed while what is *public* is exposed to general view. A woman operating in the domestic sphere *is* exposed to general view by her children, other women, and tradespeople, to name a few. Apparently, the audience, the type of spectators evoked, defines what we consider public. Further, the central act of autobiography is revelation—making public what was private. Autobiography necessitates exposure, inherently transforming any private event into public experience. Also, as Domna Stanton points out, quoting Philippe Lejeune, what do the words "private" or "personal" mean in a genre focusing on "the history of the individual personality" (13). In particular, Stanton queries, what does the word "personal" mean: "a particular type of introspective and affective analysis? a certain quantity and quality of detail?" (13). Paradoxically, for either a man or a woman, autobiography is at once personal and public as it is necessarily personal in focus and public in process.

The fragmented, disjointed style deemed characteristic of women's autobiographies is often theorized as being imitative of the disrupted "dailiness" of their actual lives. To illustrate the point, as I write this I am being continually interrupted by my young daughter. However, I am not sure it is affecting my writing style one way or another. Further, to assert that our writing emerges in direct imitation of the lives we lead assumes a mimetic fidelity at odds with autobiographical process.

Autobiography is largely an act of deletion and interruption. Confronted with the unruly array of details in our lives, we subtract. Mimesis comes into play more readily when creating a fictional character; there we add more and more material in an effort to make the character complete and life-like. An autobiographical subject, however, is already complete—too complete, in fact. Alice Jardine, speaking of another topic entirely, nevertheless offers a model of autobiographical creation when she writes, "the sculptor-subject [or autobiographer] . . . constantly moves around the material to be formed, never staying in one position very long, removing more and more material in order to create a shape . . . participating in an extreme *emptying out* of images, narrative, characters, and words, in order to reach their silent but solidly significant core—an erotic core that he can then embrace" (235).

In short, an autobiography is a selective, packaged product. The autobiographer presents a performance, shaped by his or her knowledge of fiction (a good narrative must tell a story) and the *bildungsroman* tradition of autobiography. For a woman, the culturally acceptable story of her education must often be achieved by distancing herself from her mother, whose intellectual abilities have either not been allowed to develop or have been culturally dismissed. The mother—typically—does not present a model whose power exceeds the domestic sphere; further, the mother's socially constructed connection to "body" threatens—by association—the daughter's ability to represent herself as part of autobiography's cultural/spiritual realm. Accordingly, the strategies a daughter employs to position herself in relation to her mother—strategies affected by historical, cultural, racial, and socioeconomic determinants—may be a central way to examine the difference between men and women's autobiographies.   Whether the daughter as autobiographer ultimately presents her mother negatively or positively, the mother's representation remains textually complex and problematic.

More recent studies of autobiography, besides that of Domna Stanton's, tread carefully over the ground of male and female difference in autobiography. Shari Benstock, who edited the 1988 collection of essays on women's autobiographies entitled, *The Private Self*, warns that sharply defining a woman's tradition in autobiography erases a woman's differences in history, social class, race, religion, and other concepts that define a person's identity: "The effort to theorize a paradigm of self that would include each of these women is revealed as naive and critically self-serving" (9). In another collection of essays on women's autobiographies published the same year, the editors, Bella Brodski and Celeste Schenck, articulate a similar caveat: "The establishment of a separatist female tradition, even feminist critics have warned, carries the danger of reverse reification" (*Life/Lines: Theorizing Women's Autobiography* 15).

Sidonie Smith in her book, *A Poetics of Women's Autobiography*, provides a sustained discussion about the question of difference in women's autobiographies. Smith's book, published in 1987, is one of the few full-length works treating—primarily—female autobiographical theory. After giving a historical overview of primarily male autobiographical criticism and explaining how women have been largely silenced, Smith proceeds to discuss "difference." Smith refers to the "piece by piece" effort of feminist literary critics to write "a literary history of women's self-representation" (17). Smith expresses reservations about the theories of difference elucidated by earlier women scholars who argue "that the specificity of women's autobiography comes from thematic content, determined by women's proscribed status in patriarchal culture. Instead of adventures and vocations . . . women write about the sphere of domesticity and about the affective curve in the plot of love" (17).

This argument, Smith asserts, becomes reductive: "But the recourse to a binarism that reifies the public-private opposition eventuates in a simplistic and unsatisfactory description of textual difference. Examples that bely the opposition abound" (17). Smith disputes the idea that women write in a fragmentary style that imitates their "real" lives (17) and again points out the many women who do not write in this manner.

At the same time, Smith does not deny that a woman writing an autobiography speaks from a different position than a man. However, launching any set theory of difference may encourage a static dualism; that is, the process Elizabeth L. Berg depicts as "the double move of reifying a diversity of traits into a determination of masculine or feminine, and then essentializing that determination," a step "that holds one in the hierarchy of the sexes" (qtd. in Smith 49).

Smith also points out the difficulty of women writing in a purely "female" language since a woman "must suspend herself between paternal and maternal narratives, those fictions of male and female selfhood that permeate her historical moment" (19). Smith sees the possibility of describing a woman's tradition in autobiography as inherently complex. A woman's narrative, Smith reminds us, remains caught up in both male and female cultural determinants, resulting in a "double helix of the imagination" in her autobiography where "the voices of man and woman, Adam and Eve, vie with one another, displace one another, subvert one another in the constant play of uneasy appropriation or reconciliation and daring rejection" (51). In a later passage, Smith restates her thesis of how a woman creates her autobiographical stance:

> Fashioning her own voice within and against the voices of others, she performs a selective appropriation of stories told by and about men and women. Subversively, she rearranges the dominant discourse and the dominant ideology of gender, seizing the language and its powers to turn cultural fictions into her very own story. (175)

What repeatedly surfaces in Smith's commentary is the process of positioning and strategy a woman undertakes in writing her autobiography.

Janice Morgan compiles a deliberately diverse collection of essays in her 1991 book, *Redefining Autobiography in Twentieth-Century Women's Fiction: An Essay Collection*, to promote "an expanded awareness of the social, political, and moral dimensions in which our selves are produced" (14). Similarly, Julia Watson and Sidonie Smith in their essay collection, *De/Colonizing the Subject: The Politics of Gender in Women's Autobiography* (1992), also argue for a more diverse perspective since generalizations about women exclusively in terms of their gender can serve to efface all the other oppressions women often face (xiv). Leigh Gilmore in her full-length study of autobiography, *Autobiographics: A Feminist Theory of Women's Representation* (1994) acknowledges that while men and women experience a different "lived reality" just how that difference might be theorized remains an "open question" (x). Gilmore rejects constructing a theory of "shared 'female experience'" (xi) in favor of a "feminist theory of autobiographical production"(xi) she terms "autobiographics" that would take into account the "changing elements of the contradictory discourses and practices of truth and identity which represent the subject of autobiography" (13). While Gilmore raises articulate injunctions against simplistic generalizations based on gender, it can be argued that one of the disenfranchised groups often erased in feminist discourse *are* mothers—a group difficult to discuss without reference to gender. And, as Hirsch notes, mothers could make the same claims Gilmore cites regarding marginalization and rightly denounce "daughterly feminism" as parallel to the critiques by white feminism about women of color in the United States, as well as to the similar critiques by Western feminism about Third World women and the critiques by middle-class feminism about working-class women (165). While the earlier feminist studies centering on difference were necessary to lay the foundations for further theorization, the more recent studies emphasize the complex cultural, historical, sexual positioning an autobiographical subject must undergo in representing herself.

It may be argued, too, that *both* men and women use narrative strategies and position themselves carefully when writing an autobiography; that, in fact, writing an autobiography is performative for either gender. Norrine Voss comments similarly on the complexities inherent in the genre itself, explaining that writing autobiography is difficult for both men and women since in self-revelation there is always the problem of reconciling the inner and outer person and as well as various other challenges inherent in the genre such as:

> feeling uncomfortable with the possibility of seeming conceited, and overcoming the obstacles standing in the way of telling the truth about the self. Although both sexes face these problems, women's socialization has made their experience somewhat different from men's. It is, however, a difference in *degree* rather than kind. (226, emphasis added)

Though I mostly concur with Voss's statement, I would argue that the difference between men and women's autobiographies is one of both "degree" and "kind," a point that may become clearer in the next section's discussion concerning the construction of the autobiographical subject and how it is inflected by gender.

The Autobiographical Man/The Autobiographical Woman

> Hence we find the beginning of the "chain of desire" and the chain of signifiers at the center of Lacan's psycholinguistics—the presupposition that all systems of representation are based on absence, echoing the primal loss of the mother. We begin to see, then, the dependence of both androcentric and "phallocentrism" on the loss or absence of the mother, the event that is both solicited and mourned, so that, as Terry Eagleton has written, "to enter language is to be severed from

... the mother's body .... We will spend all of our lives hunting for
it."

—Deborah Kelly Kloepfer, *The Unspeakable Mother*

As Norrine Voss explains, constructing an autobiographical subject creates problems inherent in the genre itself, largely uninflected by gender. For a man or a woman, the creation of an autobiographical self is a creation of allegory. Eric Auerbach in *Mimesis: The Representation of Reality in Western Literature* perceives allegory—in its traditional configurations—as the opposite of mimesis, of "realistic" literature (261). My own view, however, also suggested by such critics as Angus Fletcher, Gay Clifford and, in particular, Paul de Man, situates allegory in a less antithetical position to mimesis.

Autobiography, theoretically a "mimetic," non-fictional genre, necessarily operates within an allegorical mode, involving a sideways movement through the layers of self, a process of "blindness and insight," akin to the allegorizing properties of J. Hillis Miller's "lateral dance" or Paul de Man's "allegories of reading." Like the critic, surveying a literary work, the autobiographer, surveying his life, can only "see" parts of it, and selects from these parts the moments that will comprise his or her autobiography.

In a desire for narrative coherence, these moments may become linked to form a pattern. Further, the earlier events of one's life gain automatic resonance by virtue of their relation to the end or present status of the autobiographer's life. We read the highlighted moments of an autobiographer's life both forwards and back, the earlier and later events of the autobiographer's life comprising a sort of self-contained typology. Peter Brooks explains this process somewhat similarly in his book, *Reading for the Plot:*

> The sense of a beginning, then, must in some important way be determined by the sense of an ending. We might say that we are able to read present moments—in literature and, by extension, in life—as en-

dowed with narrative meaning only because we read them in antici-
pation of the structuring power of those endings that will retrospectively give them the order and significance of plot. (94)

Sartre, speaking of his autobiography in this fashion, "began to see
himself as in a book, being read by posterity 'from death to birth'; he un-
dertook to live his life retrospectively, in terms of the death that alone
would confer meaning and necessity on existence. As he most succinctly
puts it, 'I became my own obituary'" (qtd. in Brooks in passim 94–95).

In place of the subject's death or "end", necessarily impossible in
autobiography, a pronounced degree of patterning emerges to create a
"story." Rousseau, for example, highlights the moments of injus-
tice/humiliation in his life, Henry Adams the moments of (failed) education, Benjamin Franklin the moments of instructive exempla, Annie
Dillard the childhood moments of awakening consciousness, Simone de
Beauvoir the moments of (successful) education, and Maya Angelou the
alternating moments of obstruction and freedom.

Every act of selection, then—done consciously or unconsciously—
causes several instances of suppression. Whether these "highpoints" become formalistically shaped into some coherent pattern or not, the autobiographical process could not be called strictly linear or continuous. At
best, its narrative process is segmented, contiguous, metonymic, and directed toward allegory. By virtue of the selection itself, the foregrounded moments in an autobiography—reinterpreted and recon-
structed—become imbued with value and form a skeletal narrative that
both defines and cancels the self.

Whether autobiography is highly reflexive and deliberately disjointed or hides its props in an attempt at seamless mimesis, it remains
allegorical in its impulse: spatialized, fragmented, symbolic, and instructive, although here allegory's didactic function reverts back to its creator,
who learns one version of his/her life as it sifts through the net of desire,
memory, and language. That autobiography *creates* learning is similarly
articulated by Kathleen Woodward, who writes that "*knowledge*, in the

sense of *savoir*" which is associated "with the achieved understanding of one's psychic past (and present) in the psychoanalytic mode" is "crucial to autobiographical practice" (99). Given its subjectivity, that autobiography remains closer to fiction than to fact is inevitable—as Northrop Frye points out when he writes that autobiography "is another form that merges with the novel by a series of insensible gradations" (307). However earnestly we might desire to depict our life factually, it is, as Ihab Hassan explains, "impossible":

> . . . how can life come alive to itself winding in the infinite folds of its own hermeneutic circle? How can self apprehend itself in the very act of its flight from death? But deadly too in this sense: autobiography is abject unless, in the words of Michel Leiris, it exposes itself to the "bull's horn." For writing about ourselves we risk cowardice and mendacity; and more, we risk changing ourselves by that writing into whatever an autobiographer pretends to be.

As an act of exposure, then, the lure of autobiography is to lie; the risk is that we *will*, for what we write writes us in turn.

On the other hand, autobiography's dialectical teetering between mimesis and fantasy may even be desirable, creating, perhaps, a version of self that is truer by its testing and refining of the "facts." Ultimately, a person cannot begin to think about or describe his/her life *without* constructing a narrative, story that interprets and connects the facts and fictions of one's life. Gregory Jay, discussing Freud and autobiography, similarly speculates on autobiographical "truth":

> The identification of the self with the process of symbolic construc-
> tion means that a text's way of composition, rather than its narrative
> events or referents, may contain the "truer" autobiography since its
> ambivalent signifying movements enact the defenses and displace-
> ments that constitute the itinerary of identity and concept formation.
> (112)

In any case, autobiography's slippage into two genre (fiction and non-fiction) remains unavoidable and similar to the double movement Roland Barthes sees enacted in any attempt to represent reality:

> The fact that we cannot manage to achieve more than an unstable grasp of reality doubtless gives the measure of our present alienation: we constantly drift between an object and its demystification, powerless to render its wholeness. For if we penetrate the object, we liberate it but we destroy it; and if we acknowledge its full weight, we respect it, but we restore it to a state which is still mystified. ("Mythologies" 159)

The autobiographer, foregrounding certain moments in his/her existence, says, in effect: "Look at these, the important events of my life!" and then instinctively recoils from these events, realizing by acknowledging their "full weight" they will become mystified and false.

Consequently, while autobiography proceeds allegorically on a horizontal axis, it also unfolds vertically, synchronically, and here expresses itself in the form of irony. The rhetoric of irony serves to partially flatten, to lessen the weight of, the very moments/monuments allegory has erected. Paul de Man explains the criss-crossing paths of allegory and irony, a pairing of a narrative and a rhetorical mode I believe inherent in the construction of autobiography, in the "Rhetoric of Temporality":

> Irony comes closer to the pattern of factual experience and recaptures some of the factitiousness of human experience as a succession of isolated moments lived by a divided self. Essentially the mode of the present, it knows neither memory nor prefigurative duration, whereas allegory exists entirely within an ideal time that is never here or now but always a past or an endless future. Irony is a synchronic structure, while allegory appears as a successive mode capable of engendering duration as the illusion of a continuity that it knows to be illusory. (226)

Irony, then, stops time, piercing through the flow of allegory like a scalpel to unfold and critique the moments allegory has highlighted. Henry Adams and Mary McCarthy's autobiographies serve as extreme examples of this use of irony. Henry Adams (*The Education of Henry Adams*) repeatedly undercuts his carefully wrought experiences by dubbing them a failure, while Mary McCarthy pauses in each chapter of her autobiography (*Memories of a Catholic Girlhood*) to question its veracity, and at one point flatly states, "There are several dubious points in this memoir" (46).

A woman's use of allegory and irony in autobiography plays out differently in both degree and kind. For a woman, writing an autobiography intended for publication, the male *bildungsroman* model of autobiography provides her with an allegorical structure that comes pre-patterned and overdetermined. If an autobiography's trajectory is traditionally intellectual and cultural, the female autobiographer's representation of her own body and her relationship to her mother and her mother's body are placed in immediate jeopardy. What may, in fact, be the most significant aspects in a woman's childhood and adolescence can instead become erased or distorted. To read a woman's autobiography, then, it may be necessary to explore the underside of her allegory, its dark continent of conscious and unconscious blindness.

The representation of the mother actually faces a double-bind: its repression encouraged by the demands of autobiography and its role already endangered by the need for the daughter's autonomy. Jane Flax similarly depicts the conflictive nature of the mother-daughter relationship:

> Differentiation is a central issue for women because of the special character of the mother-daughter relationship. My work differs from Nancy Chodorow's on this point, since I believe the development of women's core identity is threatened and impeded by an inability to differentiate from the mother. (23)

Alternatively, in a desire to achieve autonomy as well as write a female version of the autobiographical *bildungsroman*, the daughter may differentiate her relationship to her mother right out of existence.

Accordingly, many daughters as autobiographers pay brief homage to their mothers and then dismiss them as they go on to explain how they identified with their fathers. While the daughter often describes her affiliation with her father in a tone of rebellious pride, nothing, from a Freudian standpoint, could be more traditional. As many feminists have noted, for all the theorization on the Oedipal scene, few tell Jocasta's story. The mother is silent.

When the figure of the mother is not erased entirely, she is often reduced to body. Importantly, the daughter does not present her own body but the body of her mother. The mother's body may be safely explored, and even serve as a substitute for the daughter's corporeal self without risking a direct representation of the daughter's own body. As Shirley Neuman, in her essay "Autobiography and the Construction of the Feminine Body," points out, "Bodies rarely figure in autobiography" (1). But women have always been seen as bodies. The problem, Neuman goes on to explain, effectively hamstrings a woman's ability to represent herself candidly:

> Contradictorily, a tradition of autobiography which identifies the genre with spirituality leaves the potential woman autobiographer in the position of either not writing at all, or of having to invent a self that is female and non-corporeal, which is to say, in the impossible position of inventing a self outside western cultures' inscriptions of femininity on and through her body" ("Autobiography" 2)

The body of the mother, then, becomes a simultaneous site of obsession and dis-identification. The daughter may indirectly present a corporeal self through the mother's body but then must dissociate herself from the mother in order to fulfill autobiography's traditional cultural/spiritual trajectory.

I would also speculate that women's autobiographies are both more and less ironic than men's. When Henry Adams speaks of his education in a consistently self-deprecating style, he is also speaking from a position of privilege. Certainly there is no irony in the autobiographies of Zora Neale Hurston, Maya Angelou, Simone de Beauvoir, Charlotte Perkins Gilman, Ellen Glasgow, Eudora Welty, or Harriet Martineau as they describe their intellectual achievements; the stakes simply are too high. Not surprisingly, irony, which is also a defense mechanism, does surface consistently and intensely when women write of their physical appearance, their mothers, and their domestic life.

*   *   *   *   *

This book focuses on how the figure of the mother emerges in women's autobiographies as both a textual body and a textual problem. Though much of my inquiry relies on an Oedipal, psychoanalytic model, I do not accept Freudian/Lacanian theorization without reservations. But it may not even matter. Arguing about whether the Oedipal model is true or not is moot in a society that has already incorporated Freud's concepts. Our media are saturated with images of nurturing mothers and active fathers and our society, like psychoanalysis, is intensely child-centered. From this standpoint, using a psychoanalytic model may be simply an act of cultural mirroring.

To demonstrate the strategies women have used to represent and (occasionally) assume the position of the mother, my chapters are arranged in a loose progression. "A Body Among Minds," is primarily a discussion of Simone de Beauvoir's *Memoirs of a Dutiful Daughter* and her desire to maintain a mind/body split that effects both the erasure of the mother and the effacement of her own body. Beauvoir serves as particularly extreme example of a gesture demonstrable in many women's autobiographies: the affiliation with the father at the mother's expense. In a later autobiography also discussed (*A Very Easy Death*), Beauvoir begins to re-confront her own body, her mother, and the concept of death inextricably linked to the body and the figure of the mother.

"Erotic Surfaces: The Mother as Spectacle," primarily focuses on Nathalie Sarraute and Annie Dillard to explore how the mother's body is often taken up in obsessive detail. Both Dillard and Sarraute use the body of the mother as a locus of desire on which to play out their own hungers and/or conflicts. The body of the mother is also discussed in the works of Mary McCarthy, Zora Neale Hurston, and Maya Angelou, concentrating, in particular, on what happens when the mother is absent.

"The Mother Speaks: A Really Bloody Show," treats the kinds of autobiographies mothers have produced and the strategies women use when speaking from the position of the mother. Popular autobiographers such as Erma Bombeck, Shirley Jackson, Jean Kerr, and Betty McDonald often use narrative techniques to distance themselves from their own position as mothers. Charlotte Perkins Gilman and Maxine Hong Kingston exercise similar care in writing from and about the maternal position and in works such as Gilman's *Herland* or Kingston's, *The Woman Warrior*, they transcend the (usual) maternal position altogether.

Autobiographers like Jane Lazarre, Alta, and Nancy Mairs, however, have specifically opted to confront their roles as mothers. For these women, the mother's body is foregrounded rather than erased. Nonetheless, the hesitation, ambivalence, and even guilt Lazarre, Alta, and Mairs reveal about what they write in their autobiographies makes it clear they know they are creating a new kind of literature.

"Mother, Metaphor, and Body" revisits the site of motherhood and treats the risks inherent in a daughter telling the mother's story as well as the recurrent desire of both daughters and mothers to avoid the maternal position. Paradoxically, both the desire and the avoidance of the mother textually manifest themselves by metaphorically reducing the mother to body.

In connection with the metaphorization of the mother's body feminist critics such as Luce Irigaray, Julia Kristeva, Hélène Cixous, and Jane Gallop are discussed in relation to *écriture féminine*, artistic creation, and the maternal body. The pervasiveness of the maternal metaphor, i.e., how the mother's body repeatedly becomes connected with the unknown and the unconscious in a chain of connections leading to disease and death is explored using an example from postmodern culture: the re-formulation of family following vital organ transplantation. The transplantation of vital organs ruptures our concept of the "natural" body, and bears directly on how the role of "mother" evolves as an ideological construct. Though the dynamic of organ transplantation reveals the process of maternal metaphorization still at work, the rigid concepts of the body and family may be disintegrating somewhat in our increasingly diffuse society, a positive transformation, perhaps, that may allow the mother to be perceived with less dis-ease and more complexity.

*   *   *   *   *

I was asked, provocatively, whether I would be writing this book from the position of the daughter or the mother. An interesting question. I rambled on about not wanting to take on the authorial role inherent in speaking from the mother's position, that I was not trying to present the mother as the purveyor of truth. My answer obviously was spoken from the daughter's position and revealed my own lingering fears about phallic mothers. I also thought of hedging by quoting the passage from Adrienne Rich's book, *Of Woman Born*, where she states eloquently: "We are, none of us, 'either' mothers or daughters; to our amazement, confusion, and greater complexity, we are both" (253).

Although I am sure Adrienne Rich is right, and I am always both a mother and a daughter, this study's genesis is maternal. Like Rich, I also have three sons and carefully noted their questions and speculations as well as their attitudes toward me. When my fourth child was born, a girl, I watched for differences. For some time, aside from needing to buy her a different wardrobe, there were few changes. When my daughter began to speak and make observations, however, I was struck by her endless fascination with my mannerisms, body, and attire. She revealed, early on, that she saw me as a projection of her own future, intimately connected to me in a way my sons could not be. As I continued to read women's autobiographies, it was evident that the mother-daughter relationship, for all its power and poignancy, was often absent or diluted in their texts. This book attempts to probe that lacuna.

II

A Body Among Minds

The self who writes is not the self who lives . . . the self that writes
has neither sex nor ego, like the angels.

—"Autobiography," Marge Piercy

Creating the Mind/Body Split: Simone de Beauvoir and Motherhood

A few years ago, a friend of mine spoke to me of her desire to have a
baby. She felt—being in her early thirties—she should get on with it but
would not consider being pregnant while she was still in graduate school.
When I asked her why, she responded that pregnancy made you into such
a "body," and in the environment of graduate school, she would feel like
"a body among minds."

Her fear encapsulates a number of assumptions. A mother is a
body. A body does not think. Intellectuals—graduate students, faculty,
writers—think. Mothers do not think. A woman—as a graduate student
or a professor—writes, talks, produces, *thinks* from the position of a
daughter, that is, from the position of a female body still unencumbered
enough to think.

Pregnancy or maternity, besides being a position traditionally at
odds with thought, also represents loss of control and a resultant discomfort with the body (somatophobia). Marianne Hirsch, in *The
Mother/Daughter Plot*, isolates both lack of control and somatophobia as
two areas "of avoidance and discomfort with the maternal" (165) apparent in feminist rhetoric. In *The Women's Room*, one of Marilyn French's

characters sums up pregnancy as a time when a woman loses control of her body (and, by extension, her mind) as well as her identity:

> Pregnancy is a long waiting in which you learn what it means completely to lose control over your life. There are no coffee breaks; no days off in which you regain your normal shape and self, and can return refreshed to your labors. You can't wish away even for an hour the thing that is swelling you up, stretching your stomach until the skin feels as if it will burst, kicking you from the inside until you are black and blue. You can't even hit back without hurting yourself. The condition and you are identical: you are no longer a person, but a pregnancy. (69)

With pregnancy, you are "no longer a person," you are no longer "you." Logically, the next question is, "Will you still be you when you become a mother?"

For Simone de Beauvoir the answer would be "No": pregnancy and motherhood rob a woman of her identity and her intellect. Over and over again, in her interviews and in her books, Beauvoir refers to mothers as slaves reduced to bodies and cut off from intellectual pursuits. Beauvoir's description of pregnancy, from her influential book, *The Second Sex* (1949), sounds very much like the description quoted above from *The Women's Room*. While French's character emphasizes how much pregnancy overtakes a woman's identity, Beauvoir goes further and depicts pregnancy more like a disease that ultimately annihilates a woman:

> [the fetus is] an enrichment and an injury; the fetus is a part of her body, and it is a parasite that feeds on it; she possesses it, and she is possessed by it; it represents the future and, carrying it, she feels herself vast as the world; but this very opulence annihilates her, *she feels that she herself is no longer anything.* (emphasis added, 495)

In this theorization, a woman not only loses her former identity in the process of pregnancy, but actually loses her mind, as Beauvoir illustrates when she describes the pregnant woman in less than human terms:

> . . . but in the mother-to-be the antithesis of subject and object ceases
> to exist; she and the child with which she is swollen make up together
> an equivocal pair overwhelmed by life. Ensnared by nature, the
> pregnant woman is plant and animal, a stock-pile of colloids, an incu-
> bator, an egg; she scares children proud of their young, straight bod-
> ies and makes young people titter contemptuously because she is a
> human being, a conscious and free individual who has become life's
> passive instrument. (495)

Beauvoir's perspective in the above quotation attracts comment. Though
The Second Sex is ostensibly presented as an objective critique there is
no attempt at objectivity here. In what often amounts to an emotional ti-
rade, Beauvoir relentlessly focuses on the pregnant woman's body,
equating it with an "animal" or a "stockpile of colloids" and then—rather
gratuitously—states that a pregnant woman "scares children" and makes
them "titter contemptuously." I have quoted Beauvoir's descriptions of
pregnancy at some length because I think her attitudes about the pregnant
body and the resultant disintegration of the mind and identity she sees
occurring with maternity inform her first autobiography.

In the autobiography, published in 1958 (nine years after the *Second
Sex*), Beauvoir immediately introduces her position as daughter in the
book's title: *Memoirs of a Dutiful Daughter*. But a dutiful daughter to
whom? Although one may be a daughter to a father, a mother, or both, it
seems clear Beauvoir is writing about her relationship to her mother.
The adjective "dutiful" in the title also proves ambiguous, an ambiguity
similarly noted in Leah Hewitt's study, *Autobiographical Tightropes*
(26). The English translation of the title, *Memoirs of a Dutiful Daughter*,
is not precise; a literal translation of the title, *Mémoires d'une jeune fille
rangée*, might read "Memoirs of an Orderly Daughter." And perhaps
this less elegant translation would be more accurate, for *order* and the
desire to control her life, her mind, and her body surface as the autobiography's dominant theme.

In the autobiography, Beauvoir repeatedly demonstrates that she maintains control by keeping her body and her mind distinct. Her strategy echoes Jane Flax's excellent reading of Descartes' philosophy from a feminist perspective. In her essay, "Mother-Daughter Relationships: Psychodynamics, Politics, and Philosophy," Flax posits that "Descartes' philosophy can be read as a desperate attempt to escape from the body, sexuality, and the wiles of the unconscious" (26). To show the erasure of the body evident in Cartesian thought Flax first quotes from Descartes' *Discourse on Method*, a quote that I will present in part: "so that this 'I,' that is to say, the mind by which I am what I am, is entirely distinct from the body, even that it is easier to know than the body, and moreover, that even if the body were not, it would not cease to be all that it is" (27).

Flax argues that Descartes' philosophy rests on the "denial of the body," and it therefore maintains the self is uninflected by the body and apparently "comes into the world whole and complete and, like a perpetual motion machine, clicks into operation" (27). Accordingly, the world is only perceptible through thought and concrete knowledge only attainable by mathematics and other exact sciences. This need for certainty, for a world governed by thought and precision, really indicates "a desire for control, control both of nature and of the body" (28).

Beauvoir's desire for certainty permeates her autobiographical project. Kathleen Woodward theorizes that it is not death that most terrifies and repulses Beauvoir but old age, and, similarly the bodily changes that occur with adolescence, menstruation, pregnancy, childbirth, lactation, and so forth. In short, Woodward asserts, Beauvoir's disgust rests on "an aversion to bodily transformation" (96). What motivates Beauvoir's aversion to bodily transformations, I would posit, is that they defy control. The flow of menstrual blood, the body's "swelling up" in pregnancy, the rush of fluids in childbirth, the flow of milk when nursing, the wrinkled and drooping skin of old age all represent changes in the body that occur spontaneously, beyond intellectual control. The only changes Beauvoir could control were those associated with pregnancy and motherhood. Accordingly, Beauvoir consciously chose not to have children, a choice Woodward also sees as suggestive: "Surely it is not insignificant that neither as an adolescent nor as an adult did she see motherhood as part of her future" (104).

Not surprisingly, Beauvoir's rather hostile attacks on motherhood—particularly in *The Second Sex*—have incited many feminist debates. As Deirdre Bair notes in her book, *Simone de Beauvoir: A Biography* (1990), the initial reactions to *The Second Sex* by writers such as Margaret Mead, Stevie Smith, Katherine Anne Porter, or Elizabeth Hardwick focused on the book's lack of objectivity and, in the words of Stevie Smith, Beauvoir's apparent dismay with her gender: "Miss de Beauvoir has written an enormous book about women, and it is soon clear that she does not like them and does not like being a woman" (qtd. in Bair 438). Conversely, other writers/feminists such as Sharon Firestone or Kate Millett found Beauvoir's theories so influential that they "modeled their radical feminism on *The Second Sex*" (Simons 9). As Margaret A. Simons points out, though, in her introduction to *Feminist Interpretations of Simone de Beauvoir* (1995), from the late 1960s until after Beauvoir's death in 1986, the book underwent "intense feminist criticism" due to its purported male-defined phenomenological and existential stance (9). Since 1986, Simons argues, feminists have reinterpreted Beauvoir more complexly and more favorably. Feminist critics such as Karen Vintges, Michèle Le Doeuff, Sonia Kruks, or Debra Bergoffen from Simons' book or Toril Moi from her book, *Simone de Beauvoir: The Making of an Intellectual Woman* (1994) re-examine her works in light of the social, political, and philosophical climate in which Beauvoir wrote. While these critics provide intelligent rebuttals to claims that Beauvoir's theories are phallocentric, elitist, ahistorical, apolitical, masculinist, etc., none of these interpretations of Beauvoir fully succeed in justifying Beauvoir's consistently disparaging comments on motherhood.

Although Yolanda Patterson credits Beauvoir with "demystifying" motherhood (*Simone de Beauvoir and the Demystification of Motherhood*), what may have been accomplished might be more accurately described as a "remystification" (105). Rather than merely exposing maternity as a site of potential patriarchal oppression and a position that has often been overly romanticized, Beauvoir re-creates motherhood into a powerfully negative myth. In Beauvoir's theorization motherhood is a double-trap because women who succumb to motherhood become trapped and, in turn, mothers *en*trap—literally devour—their children, e.g., "[a woman is] a swamp in which insects and children are engulfed" (Beauvoir qtd. in Léon 144–45). While it could be argued that her views toward motherhood, particularly in *The Second Sex*, represent an earlier view, Beauvoir never retracts these statements. As late as 1984—two years before her death—Beauvoir gave the following response when Hélène V. Wenzel asked her what she thought about the "motherhood issue" and whether she saw these "questions about maternity" as "important":

> All questions are important. But, well, from all that I have seen, it appears that mother/daughter relationships are generally bad. No matter what the mother does, because . . . the mother wants to be a friend at the same time. As she also wants to be the one to direct her daughter. Well, I've really seen some very unfortunate relationships between mothers and daughters. (26)

Again, what surprises here is Beauvoir's inability to view a mother's role as anything but negative. While Patterson lauds Beauvoir for seeing as early as 1949 the often destructive powers of motherhood "much literature and film footage" has only begun to see, Patterson does not note that this is *all* Beauvoir sees (89). Never, in any of her works, is Beauvoir able to view motherhood as a positive value, as an option a woman might willingly choose. For Beauvoir, as Dorothy Kaufman similarly notes, the "maternal, even as metaphor, will always look to Beauvoir like a trap, in which women lose their autonomy and their happiness" (126). In an effort to elude this trap, Beauvoir chooses the life of the mind, the life she feels she can control.

While Beauvoir is ultimately betrayed by her body—it changes with adolescence and aging—she could discipline her mind. Early in the autobiography, Beauvoir expresses her excitement as she discovers the joy of books and knowledge. Evident in her description, is the pleasure she takes in education as a means for autonomy and control, as a time when she would have a life of her "own" where here "days and weeks would be arranged according" to her "own timetable" (21).

Beauvoir's focus on what she may control and order by her intellect so influences her autobiography that it becomes a terrain of the mind, curiously drained of any physical "landscapes, furnishings, dresses . . . traits that characterize a period, speak of a social climate" (Roy 81). Significantly, Beauvoir enjoys most the visions she can manipulate and control: "Shadow theatres, magic lanterns: what interested me in all these optical illusions was that they were the product of my own eyes " (23).

Her early idolization of her mother is largely described in terms of the pleasure she derives from her mother's firm, young body: "I would sit upon her knees, enclosed by the perfumed softness of her arms, and cover with kisses her fresh, youthful skin" (6). She also bonds with her mother in "pious collusion" as the two plot out her religious course (30). Beauvoir's mother guides her spiritual growth and Simone works hard at staging her religious persona, a manipulation she also views ironically (although the irony probably reflects the *adult* autobiographer's perspective):

> I had made a definite metamorphosis into a good little girl. Right from the start, I had composed the personality I wished to present to the world; it had brought me so much praise and so many great satisfactions that I had finished by identifying myself with the character I had built up: it was my one reality. (30)

Though Beauvoir's early descriptions of her mother appear positive, the reduction of her mother to a beautiful body and moral guide reflects a predictable social pattern.

The commodification of maternity—ostensibly a celebration of motherhood—really serves to keep the mother in her place. The packaged mother—beautiful, nurturing and self-sacrificing—elicits adoration, devotion, and guilt. Not surprisingly, Mother's Day prompts consumers to spend more money per gift than they do for any other "holy" day all year. Centuries of paintings of Madonna and child and/or mother and child, as well as verse written at the level of greeting card rhetoric reinforce the notion of what a mother should be. The passive specularity of the mother—idols should be stationary—serves also to contain the mother by defining her position in the nature/culture binary. Connected to nature, the mother becomes body, while the father, associated with culture, becomes mind. The mother's body *warrants* the daughter's adoring gaze because she, in turn, gazes adoringly at her and fulfills her bodily needs. The daughter's cultural needs, apparently, must be met elsewhere.

In a key passage in the *Memoirs*, Beauvoir outlines this nature/culture, maternal/paternal split as she describes her relationship with her father:

> . . . to him I was neither body nor soul, but simply a mind. Our relationship was situated in a pure and limpid atmosphere where unpleasantness could not exist. He did not condescend to me, but raised me up to his level . . . . When I fell back to my ordinary level, I was dependent upon Mama; Papa had allowed her to take complete charge of my bodily and moral welfare. (37)

Every important male relationship Beauvoir depicts in the *Memoirs* could be described in much the same terms: as an association of minds. Beauvoir's desire to join with the father in a collusion of minds and turn away from the regressive aspects she sees literally em(bod)ied in the mother, echo the daughter's voice in Luce Irigaray's essay, "And the One Doesn't Stir Without the Other":

I'll turn to my father. I'll leave you for someone who seems more alive than you. For someone who doesn't prepare anything for me to eat. For someone who leaves me empty of him, mouth gaping on his truth. I'll follow him with my eyes, I'll listen to what he says, I'll try to walk behind him. He leaves the house, I follow in his steps. Farewell, Mother, I shall never become your likeness. (62)

Over and over again, in women's autobiographies, we may observe this same movement. Metaphorically or otherwise, the daughter associates the "active" part of her identity—her mind, of course—with her father and, in essence, waves good-bye to her mother. If the daughter does not actually dissociate from her mother, the attention she gives to depicting her mother's body versus her father's mind accomplishes the same thing. Carolyn G. Heilbrun in her book, *Writing a Woman's Life*, similarly notes the sharp division daughters draw between their fathers and mothers. After reading a number of autobiographical essays (written from the daughter's point of view), Heilbrun states that "one may generalize from these essays with minor, if any, exaggeration that fathers are the pivot" that incite their daughters intellectual awakening while, in contrast, "Mothers have no obvious role in this change . . ." (64). Consistently, daughters (as autobiographers) emphasize their father's intellect, his library, his sense of adventure, and his books in contrast to their mother's beauty, submissiveness, and/or lack of intellect.   A medley of autobiographical voices may serve to illustrate the pattern:

Edith Wharton:

> *Peopling the background of these earliest scenes there were the tall splendid father who was always so kind, and whose strong arms lifted one so high, and my mother, who wore such beautiful flounced dresses . . . and all the other dim impersonal attributes of a Mother . . . . (26)*

My mother, herself so little of a reader, was exaggeratedly scru-
pulous about the books I read; not so much the "grown-up"
books as those written for children. (51)

Whenever I try to recall my childhood it is in my father's library
that it comes to life. (69)

Eleanor Munro:

In his enormous, windowless office at the museum, surrounded
by thousands of volumes on all the works of man . . . our father
was daily self-elevated out of self-doubt's way to a Confucian
degree of serenity. That office, all those years, filled me with
dread and gluttony. So many books, to each of which he had the
key and correct point of view! My ignorance, by contrast, felt
bottomless. My feeling about books in general, therefore,
became like that of Tantalus toward water. I thirsted for them,
to take them in with underlinings, margins notes, and endpaper
indexes which, taken all together, conceal at their core the small
grey-suited figure of my father at his desk. (124)

Hsieh Ping-Ying:

When he [her father] was only seven or eight years of age he
gained an immense love of reading. Every day when he went to
look after the cow he always took books with him . . . . So even
when I was a tiny little girl spending most of my time in my
father's arms, I was taught to read classical poetry and essays
by old masters.
As for my mother she had a very strong personality . . . . She also
had the fixed idea that the man is higher than the woman. (29,
31)

Eudora Welty:

> *In the "library," inside the mission-style bookcase with its three diamond-latticed glass doors, with my father's Morris chair and the glass-shaded lamps on its table beside it, were books I could soon begin on—and I did, reading them all alike and as they came, straight down their rows, top shelf to bottom shelf. (288)*

Maeve Binchy:

> *Whereas my father was very much the intellectual and was always getting us to study for exams and to read, my mother thought people were all important. (4)*

> *My father always encouraged us to read. He had a study where he kept all his law books; but he had quite a collection of other books . . . . My mother was not a great reader . . . . (5)*

Eva Hoffman:

> *Now I get to taste how such speed feels on my body, for as soon as he learns how to operate the motorcycle, my father picks me as his first companion for an outing to the country. Over my mother's worried protestations, I climb on the large seat behind him . . . . I'm not afraid of a real accident—I have too much confidence for that—and the truth is I like being treated like my father's buddy, and I come back flushed with wind and triumph. (10–11)*

Lillian Hellman:

> *I was puzzled and irritated by the passivity of my mother . . . . Mama seemed to do only what my father wanted. (113)*

Elizabeth Bowen:

> *True to their natures as man and woman, he was the more*
> *thoughtful, she the more feeling one. His mind had been formed*
> *by learning unknown to her: he lived by philosophy, she lived by*
> *temperament. His forehead, his talk, his preoccupations, were*
> *unmistakably those of an intellectual man . . . . As for her,*
> *because of her grace and vagueness, as well as her evident*
> *pleasure in the pretty and gay, she would not have been called*
> *an intellectual woman . . . . (41)*

Rosamond Lehmann:

> *He* [her father] *was very . . . Greek: an athlete as well as an*
> *intellectual. (150)*

> *There was a sense that I was bound to write. I never considered*
> *anything else as a possibility for my future. And I remember*
> *beginning to write stories almost as soon as I could write . . . .*
> *Everything I wrote was for my father, and shown to him. (151)*

Elizabeth Cady Stanton:

> *Then and there I resolved that I would . . . study and strive to be*
> *at the head of all my classes and thus delight my father's heart.*
> *All that day and far into the night I pondered the problem of boy-*
> *hood. I thought that the chief thing to be done in order to equal*
> *boys was to be learned and courageous. (21)*
> Note from Estelle Jelinek's *The Tradition of Women's Autobiog-*
> *raphy:*

> *Ellen Dubois, who has specialized in Stanton's life and work,*
> *notes that nothing among Stanton's papers indicates her feelings*

about her mother. (209)

Ellen Gilchrist:

I like men because they protect me. All my life they have pro-
tected me and I believe they will go on doing it as long as I love
them in return. (152)

There is an old gorgeous man living right here in Jackson, Mis-
sissippi, that I have been loving and fighting with and showing
off for since I was born fifty-one years ago. My mother's only
husband. (155)

Phyllis Shand Allfrey:

My father was literary and my mother was just a darling.
Literature was very important to me and I devoured my father's
books. (222)

Polly Devlin:

My father is an extraordinary man, a man who inspires affection.
As a child, I loved him passionately. Every passage in All of Us
There *about my father is obviously a central axis from which I*
spin. (40)

Mary Lavin:

To me he [her father] was a heroic figure and the only genius I
ever knew . . . . I always assume that any gifts I have inherited
came from my father because of the real depth and power of his
emotion . . . and yet, looking back on it, I think that I may be

*unjust to my mother, because I thought of her as such a giddy
little person, full of stories. (85)*

Anzia Yezierska:

After sending her father the book she had written:
*The pride in the new book filled me with a longing to see my
father. Because I had fought him and broken away from him as
a child, I was drawn to him as an adult, now that I was achieving
my own place in the world . . . . I found him in his room, bent
over the table with his books . . . . [he] peered at me . . . ."Only
in America could it happen [her father said]—an ignorant thing
like you—a writer! What do you know of life? Of history,
philosophy? What do you know of the Bible, the foundation of
all knowledge?" (216)*

Zora Neale Hurston:

*. . . . once I found the use of my feet, they took to wandering. I
always wanted to go . . . . This alarmed my mother a great deal
. . . . I don't know why it never occurred to her to connect this
tendency with my father, who didn't have a thing on his mind but
this town and the next one. That should have given her a sort of
hint. Some children are just bound to take after their fathers in
spite of a woman's prayers.*

**Henry Handel Richardson [Ethel Florence Lindsay (Richardson)
Robertson]:**

*I can also recall my father setting me down to passages in
Scott's novels that he thought might interest an eight-year-old. d
he lived, I should certainly have profited by his guidance. (23)*

My mother had no intellectual interests, I cannot remember ever seeing her read anything but a light novel . . . . Her talents were purely practical; and there was little she could not do with her large, capable hands. (4)

After describing her father:
Here, however, I think it only fair to add that the person who knew me best always maintained that, in my imaginary portrait of Richard Mahony [her father], *I had drawn no other than my own. (24)*

Charlotte Perkins Gilman:

By heredity I owe him [her father] *much; the Beecher urge to social service, the Beecher wit and gift of words and such small sense of art as I have . . . . (6)*

Describing her mother:
Absolutely loyal, as loving as a spaniel which no ill treatment can alienate, she made no complaint . . . . (9)

Delva Murphy:

What with my father being a librarian and Pappa plundering the bookshops of London on the Dublin quays on my behalf, I could never escape from books. Not that I wanted to. My vision of heaven was then (and still is) an infinite library. (119)

Florence King:

What they [her father and mother] *talked about over their dinner dates is unimaginable because they had absolutely nothing in common. Both had left school at fifteen but Mama quit because she hated school, while Herb's termination was decided for him by the rigid caste system of Edwardian England. Mama never read a book; Herb was a compulsive reader who had educated himself with a library card . . . . Had he become shipwrecked on a desert island he would have become, like the Birdman of Alcatraz, a self-taught expert in natural history. (17)*

Daphne Du Maurier:

. . . I liked I D[ad] *better than M*[other] (which must never be said) . . .

D[ad], *suddenly interested in our progress, produced for our enlightenment some forty small books on the Old Masters, fully illustrated, and to test our knowledge would open then at random* [and quiz Daphne and her siblings] *. . . . Poor Darling M*[other], *was I a trial to her? . . . . Could it be that, totally unconscious of the fact, she resented the ever growing bond between D*[ad] *and myself? (18, 59, 66)*

Kathleen Dayus:

And I loved me Dad. Yeah, I loved me Dad. He loved me, too . . . He was ever so good to me.
Me Dad I think was a bit above Mother because he was—he knew how to converse with people, he could talk, and everybody admired and respected him . . . . He taught me a lot Dad did. I think somehow my Dad must have had something in him, like to inspire me, because he was a scholar. I mean, he was a good scholar, he could write and he could read . . . . But Mother was very hard, very hard. (64)

Mary-Lou Weisman:

> *Sometimes I think the answer to Freud's question, "What do women want?" is Daddy. (36)*

> *I know my mother and I conspired to keep my father larger than life . . . . I wooed him with birthday poems, knock-knock jokes and good report cards. We kept each other in a female-engendered, deferential thrall to The Big Man. (7)*

What surfaces in all these quotations is how eagerly the daughter attempts to locate similarities between her father and herself. In nearly every example given above, the daughter credits her interest in learning, adventure, and literature to her father—the unquestioned site of logos. Beauvoir's life, correspondingly, reads like the parade of the fathers: her own father, the suave chaplain at the Cours Désir, her brilliant cousin Jacques Laiguillon, Robert Garric, Pierre Nodier, Pierre Clairaut, Paul Nizan, André Herbaud (René Maheu), and, of course, Jean-Paul Sartre. With the exception of Zaza Mabille, to whom I will return later, the women in Beauvoir's autobiography recede into the background. While Beauvoir's *actual* relations with women may have been quite central, consistently women are edited out of her autobiography. Further, Beauvoir's intellectual achievements place her in an elite group that at that time was almost exclusively male. Accordingly, unlike the men Beauvoir portrays, the women in her autobiography are consistently seen as lacking in intellect and "mind," a point Mary Evans articulates similarly:

> In reading de Beauvoir's account of her childhood and her adolescence in *Memoirs of a Dutiful Daughter* it is striking how strongly there emerges an association of women with all that is superstitious, petty, narrow minded, domestic, trivial, uneducated and ignorant. (182)

The roots of Beauvoir's woman/man, nature/culture dualism stem, as she consistently reminds us, from her perception of her mother and father: "I grew accustomed to the idea that my intellectual life—embodied by my father—and my spiritual life—expressed by my mother—were two radically heterogeneous fields of experience which had nothing in common" (41).

To reach the "field of experience" embodied by the mind and her father, Beauvoir must sever herself from her mother and the spiritual life she represents. Not surprisingly, Beauvoir soon discovers she no longer believes in God. Importantly, her revelation comes at a time when she is losing control of her body.

Beauvoir describes her puberty as a "difficult patch" and becomes so embarrassed by her body's changes she develops physical phobias— nervous tics—that also defy her intellectual control. On one occasion, when she gets ready to go to a wedding, a dress that formerly fit her now exposes her "breasts in an obscene fashion" (102). Her mother's solution is unfortunate, reinforcing Beauvoir's perception of adolescence as aberrant. In an attempt to get the dress to fit, her mother tries to force Beauvoir's breasts back into childlike contours: "They were then swathed in bandages and firmly flattened, so that all day I had the feeling I was concealing in my bodice some uncomfortable physical disability" (102).

During this same time, Beauvoir's father rejects her, a rejection she sees tied to her changing body: "when I entered the 'difficult' age, he was disappointed in me: he appreciated elegance and beauty in women" (107). Of interest here is the shift in perspective. Previously, according to Beauvoir, her father's approval of her was based on her intellect. In the passage above, however, her father is judging her body. Significantly, Beauvoir—though trying to deny her physical self—lets herself be judged as a body and seems as disappointed as her father that her appearance is not elegant and beautiful.

Consequently, though Beauvoir can do nothing about her own body, she can distance herself from her mother and the bodily/moral sphere she represents. Beauvoir's break with God signals her complete break with her mother. We might have intuited Beauvoir's loss of faith veiled her renewed affiliation with her father and the intellectual sphere she sees men dominating, but she spells this out. Beauvoir describes the enabling effect of her father's religious cynicism and how her rejection of religion parallels her rejection of her body, her sex: "My father's [religious] skepticism had prepared the way for me" (37). By adopting her father's religious views Beauvoir feels "great relief" since her break with religion signals her break with "the bonds of sex and childhood" as well as her affiliation with the "liberal spirits" she admired (37).

Although the spiritual is generally linked with the intellectual in traditional autobiographies, her father's skeptical view of religion encourages Beauvoir to see religion as bourgeois and mundane. In this instance, Beauvoir's rejection of religion amounts to an act of intellectual sophistication as well as serving to distance her further from her mother. Somewhat predictably, the rest of Beauvoir's autobiography largely presents a litany of her intellectual achievements. Correspondingly, as Beauvoir's world increasingly empties of physical content, the evocative, sensual prose that punctuates the beginning of the book drops away as well. As Beauvoir's education accelerates, she also distances herself from other women, finding her girlfriends "dull and stupid" (174), viewing their desire to marry with abhorrence, and seeing in their futures the destructive trajectory Hélène Cixous outlines (initially quoting James Joyce):

'Bridebed, childbed, bed of death' . . . Woman's voyage: as a *body*. As if she were destined—in the distribution established by men (separated from the world where cultural exchanges are made and kept in the wings of the social stage when it is a case of History)—to be the nonsocial, nonpolitical, non-human half of the living structure. (564)

For Beauvoir, however, her "woman's voyage" will not be done as a *body* but as a mind.

A Mind of One's Own: *Memoirs of a Dutiful Daughter*

Inherent in Beauvoir's desire to live a life of pure mind is the notion that thought and body may be kept distinct. As discussed above, women—in general—are seen as bodies and no woman is seen as more of a body than a mother: "the figure of mother is determined by her body more intensely than the figure of woman" (Hirsch 12). In intellectual discourse, few women, therefore, will foreground their sexuality and rarely—if ever—will a woman speak from the mother's position. I certainly didn't. I knew, particularly in competitively intellectual atmosphere of graduate school and academia, I should speak from the position of the [father's] daughter—the more sophisticated less embodied position. For Beauvoir, trying to gain status as an intellectual *woman* in France during the 1930s, being perceived as any *body*—daughter or mother—posed risks.

But can one really separate the mind from the body? Jean-François Lyotard provocatively explores this question in his essay, "Can Thought Go On Without a Body?" Lyotard considers whether technology could create machines "to make thinking materially possible" after our bodies are destroyed (77). Lyotard concludes that not only is thought impossibly entwined with the body but that the body actually creates thought: "Thinking and suffering overlap" (82). Thought, Lyotard posits, attempts to create endings, to once and for all silence the discomfort of the unthought:

> The unthought hurts. It's uncomfortable because we're comfortable in what's already thought. And thinking, which is accepting this discomfort, is also, to put it bluntly, an attempt to have done with it. That's the hope sustaining all writing (painting, etc.): that at the end, things will be better. As there is no end, this hope is illusory. (84)

The impasse of artificial intelligence thus hinges on desire: thought without body has no impetus. Indeed, Lyotard questions why machines designed to mimic human minds would ever *start* thinking without the discomfort of the unthought making "their memory suffer" (85). We need, he continues, "machines that suffer from the burden of their memory" (85), i.e., machines with bodies.

But it is precisely this burden, the burden of memory, the burden of the body, Beauvoir hopes to silence as she fashions her life into a trajectory of pure intellect. Increasingly, Beauvoir identifies herself with the life of the mind she associates with the male sphere while simultaneously excising all that connects her to her female body, her mother and the domestic, non-cultural sphere the mother represents.

Beauvoir's desire to not let the two spheres—that of body and that of mind—overlap, may be demonstrated as she describes the onset of puberty. When Beauvoir begins to menstruate she is appalled when her mother confides this information to her father:

> I had imagined that the monstrous regiment of women kept its blemish a secret from the male fraternity. I thought of myself in relationship to my father as a purely spiritual being: I was horrified at the thought that he suddenly considered me to be a mere organism. I felt as if I could never hold up my head again. (101)

For Beauvoir, the phrase "hold up my head" is appropriately phallic and not merely an expression. She means, quite literally, to achieve transcendence—superiority—via her mind, her "head," in a culture she sees dominated by male minds.

Beauvoir measures her success by how well she assimilates into a male world. Previously when Beauvoir had passed by the College Stanislas she viewed the college as a male domain hopelessly out of her reach. Her pride, then, is obvious as she describes her first experiences teaching at Stanislas: "now here I was out in front of the class, and it was I who was giving the lessons. I felt that there was nothing in the world I couldn't attain now" (295).

Evident in Beauvoir's autobiographical project is her need to concretize her intellectual achievements. Repeatedly she speaks of learning within the framework of a material economy where knowledge may be stored up—like money—or passed on to people less intellectually endowed. Accordingly, shortly before she takes the final examinations at the Sorbonne, she writes in her journal of the intellectual wealth she has amassed and its material value to others: "'Curious certainty that this reserve of riches that I feel within me will make its mark, that I shall utter words that will be listened to, that this life of mine will be a well-spring from which others will drink" (331)

Equally at stake in Beauvoir's autobiography is her desire to portray maternity, motherhood, and the female body as destructive, even deadly. Motherhood, marriage, the voyage of women she sees as "body," is the course Beauvoir has not chosen. Beauvoir, aptly, describes her choice to live a life of the mind—a life at odds with her bourgeois society—in markedly disembodied terms. Beauvoir describes how she rejects her physical environment in order "to enter that society . . . in which all those minds that are interested in finding out the truth communicate with each other across the distances of time and space" (282). Ironically, as Jane Flax points out, the search for truth in the world of pure mind ultimately leads right back to the body:

> The self, which is constituted by thought and created by an act of thought, by the separation of mind and body, is driven to master nature, because the self cannot ultimately deny its material character or dependence on nature. Despite Descartes' claim, the body reasserts itself, at least at the moment of death. (28)

And at the center of *Memoirs of a Dutiful Daughter* is death. If the overt allegory of Beauvoir's autobiography treats the story of her successful education, death and the maternal body emerge as its subtext. The most impassioned moments in Beauvoir's emotionally cool autobiography occur when she contemplates her own death. Through a series of displacements death repeatedly becomes associated with the body of the mother. Mothers kill. Dutiful daughters die. Wallace Stevens' line inverts to read "Mother is the death of beauty."

Beauvoir's attack on motherhood and, in particular, the destructive nature of the mother-daughter relationship may be evidenced in both the *Memoirs* and her earlier study, *The Second Sex*. In the *Second Sex*, Beauvoir's chapter on "The Mother" proves particularly revealing. Beauvoir's research in this chapter, though ostensibly objective and backed by evidence from broad samplings, rests largely on her observations of a few friends, quotes from novels and her own personal life. Beauvoir, for instance, posits that the nausea women suffer in pregnancy demonstrates that pregnancy is not a natural state for *human* women since nausea is "unknown for other mammals" (498). In evidence for this conclusion, Beauvoir pre-emptively cites herself, referring the reader to an earlier point in her own text.

Beauvoir's depiction of the mother-daughter relationship is equally unsupported and intensely autobiographical. In her *Memoirs*, Beauvoir describes how her mother meticulously controls her moral course, her choice of books, her clothes, and so forth, refusing, in essence, to grant Simone any autonomy. Beauvoir writes of the mother-daughter relationship in parallel terms in the *Second Sex*: "The pleasure of feeling absolutely superior—which men feel in regard to women—can be enjoyed by woman only in regard to her children, especially her daughters; she feels frustrated if she has to renounce her privilege, her authority" (519).

In the *Memoirs*, Beauvoir describes how her mother is her "real rival" and hinders her ability to have an "intimate relationship" with her father (107). Yolanda Patterson, discussing the *Memoirs*, writes that Beauvoir "was convinced her mother dressed her in unattractive clothes in order to keep her asexual as long as possible" (156). Similarly, Beauvoir writes in the *Second Sex*: "Frequently the oldest girl [like Simone], her father's favorite, is the special object of the mother's persecution . . . .she keeps the girl in the house, watches her, tyrannizes over her; she purposely dresses her like a fright" (519, 520). Clearly, the mother-daughter relationship outlined in the *Second Sex* does not portray mothers and daughters in general, but the *specific* relationship Beauvoir experienced with her own mother.

Though controlling mothers, such as Françoise de Beauvoir, prove destructive, Zaza's mother—as Beauvoir would have us believe—proves deadly. It is Beauvoir's close friend, Zaza, who is the autobiography's real "dutiful daughter." Although Beauvoir's friendship with Zaza seems well developed and integral to the action in the middle of the book, her character becomes more tangential as Beauvoir's attention increasingly turns to her studies at the Sorbonne. It is only at the very end of the autobiography, as Zaza's relationship with Jean Pradelle (Maurice Merleau-Ponty) becomes stalled, that Beauvoir again makes Zaza the book's central focus. Unexpectedly, for Zaza's character has been portrayed as volatile throughout, Zaza becomes ill with "meningitis, encephalitis; no one was quite sure" (360) and dies. Rather abruptly, Beauvoir's *Memoirs* end as well, with only a jarringly odd final line offered in dénouement: "We [Zaza and Beauvoir] had fought together against the revolting fate that had lain ahead of us, and for a long time I believed that I had paid for my own freedom with her death" (360).

Zaza's death shatters all Beauvoir's preconceptions. Earlier, when Beauvoir hears of her grandfather's imminent death, she reacts to the news calmly, even somewhat coldly. Beauvoir remarks that her grandfather was very ill and very old so that his death "seemed natural" and she "could feel no sadness about it" (317). Zaza's death, on the other hand, is not natural. If a young brilliant girl could die without warning none of Beauvoir's carefully wrought plans held any certainty—if Zaza's death were meaningless then life could be meaningless as well.

Zaza's death, Beauvoir thus suggests, is caused by making the wrong choice: the daughter who stays dutiful to her mother dies, the one who doesn't wins her freedom. Zaza's mother, of course, is the villain. Madame Mabille, whose permissiveness initially impresses Beauvoir, actually proves more formidable than Françoise de Beauvoir. Madame Mabille's greater subtlety makes her infinitely more dangerous. Beauvoir describes how Madame Mabille controls Zaza and her other children by a "clever policy" in which she gives in to her children for small things so that "when it was a question of getting them to do something her credit was unimpaired" (280). In this description, Beauvoir again resorts to economic metaphors. Like Beauvoir's intelligence that may be saved and invested, Madame Mabille stores up good will through her permissiveness until it is time to call in the loan. Beauvoir similarly commodifies Zaza when she ends her autobiography by stating that she "had paid for" her freedom with Zaza's death.

In the check and balance of Beauvoir's economic system the mother's body is a debit that leads to death. Every fit of anguish Beauvoir experiences over the prospect of death rotates around the body of her mother. By making Zaza's death the climactic moment of her autobiography, Beauvoir suggests she only narrowly escapes a similar fate by breaking away from her own mother. Early in the autobiography, Beauvoir's first intuition of death occurs when her mother feeds her, spoonful by spoonful while warning, "If you don't eat anything, you won't grow up into a big girl" (7). But becoming a big girl, Beauvoir realizes would also distance herself from the body of her mother ("I won't be able to sit on her knee any more.") and Beauvoir senses that the future has risks. With the future, Beauvoir would age and turn into someone who would both be, and not be, herself. Beauvoir suddenly has "forebodings of the separations" and "of the long succession of [her] various deaths" (7).

The body of the mother again emerges in the chain of thought leading to death when Beauvoir reads a fairy tale. Beauvoir suddenly realizes that if her mother gave birth to her there was also a time before her birth when she did not exist. Pre-birth equaled death: "In the darkness of the past . . . I had dire forebodings of my own extinction" (49).

When Beauvoir effects her break with her mother by rejecting religion, she finds that in losing God she is alone and condemned to death. Beauvoir becomes hysterical and describes how she screamed and "tore at the red carpet" (138). In a later scene, Beauvoir again depicts her fear of death, of "nothingness," as she lies alone in bed. In both instances, she tells how she wants to rush back to her mother "just in order to hear a human voice" (207).

The body of the mother, Beauvoir senses, is a site of ambivalence: in giving life mothers also ensure death. For Beauvoir, this included metaphorical deaths as well: choosing the life of the body—the mother—would kill the life of the mind. As Alice Jardine comments, speaking of Beauvoir's either/or economy, it was always "the baby [motherhood] *versus* the book . . . . In the classical feminist economy, you cannot have them both; you cannot have it all" (90). Accordingly, for Beauvoir, the mother represents all that is on the right side of the male/female binary: activity/passivity, culture/nature, day/night, logos/pathos, mind/body. In short, as "Bataille knew, and Cixous reminds us, the fear of the right side of the binary is the fear of death itself" (Latimer 558). In *A Very Easy Death*, Beauvoir finally confronts this fear.

Her Mother/Her Self: *A Very Easy Death*

> If there is no true recognition of the mother's part, then there must remain a vague fear of dependence. This fear will sometimes take the form of a fear of women in general or fear of a particular woman, and at other times will take on less easily recognized forms, always including the fear of domination.
>
> —D.W. Winnicott (qtd. in Benjamin 206)

I encountered *A Very Easy Death* twice before actually reading it. The two encounters amounted to radically different readings of the same text. My first encounter with *A Very Easy Death* was not exactly a reading but an abridgment of the book that appeared in an anthology entitled *Mothers: Memories, Dreams and Reflections by Literary Daughters* edited by Susan Cahill. The collection aims to present an array of well-known women writers' memories of their mothers depicted in "positive tones and vivid colors" (xii). The selection from Beauvoir's book, *A Very*

Easy Death, recounts her mother's death from cancer. Despite the general excellence of the anthology, I later found the abridgment of Beauvoir's text amounted to a bowdlerization: the less positive aspects of their mother-daughter relationship, and Beauvoir's more explicit descriptions—the body parts, the private parts—had all been removed.

Though much of the text is necessarily shortened to accommodate an anthology format, many of the omissions are telling. In the first third of the book, Beauvoir's reactions to her mother's impending death are highly ambivalent; initially, many of her comments seem more callous than caring. Accordingly, this entire section is deleted. In a later section that is included, a single paragraph is omitted, apparently because Beauvoir's clinical descriptions of her mother's illness jar with the poignant tone the editor is trying to establish. The omitted paragraph is quoted in part:

> With the removal of the filth that had swollen her abdomen the day before, she was no longer in pain . . . . Thanks to the transfusions and the infusions Maman's face had some colour again and a look of health. The poor suffering thing that had been lying on the bed the day before had turned back into a woman. (46)

In another instance, only the last line in a paragraph is omitted. The anthology includes Poupette's [Beauvoir's sister] words: "'If she has a few days of happiness like this, keeping her alive will have been worth while,' said Poupette to me" (Cahill 32) and then omits Beauvoir's aside: "But what was it going to cost?" (50). The rest of the book, describing her mother's brutal illness and death, is also omitted. Only the final pages of the book, where Beauvoir writes movingly of her mother's death and death in general, are again included.

My second encounter with *A Very Easy Death* occurred when reading an article by Alice Jardine entitled "Death Sentences: Writing Couples and Ideology." It was Jardine's article that prompted me to go back to Beauvoir's original text, because none of the quotes Jardine cited had appeared in the anthologized version of *A Very Easy Death*. Unlike Susan Cahill, who edited the anthology to conform to more sentimental notions of motherhood, Jardine focuses specifically on how Beauvoir's mother is "buried in and by narrative" (93), on Beauvoir's clinically explicit descriptions of her mother's cancerous, decomposing body.

In particular, Jardine cites the passage where Beauvoir has walked into the hospital room and suddenly sees her mother exposed by her open hospital nightdress. The garment gapes, but not to show, as Roland Barthes would posit, the "(absent, hidden, or hypostatized) father" (10), but the mother:

> Maman had an open hospital nightdress on and she did not mind that her wrinkled belly, criss-crossed with tiny lines, and her bald pubis showed." I no longer have any sort of shame," she observed in a surprised voice.
>
> "You are perfectly right not to have any," I said. But I turned away and gazed fixedly into the garden. The sight of my mother's nakedness had jarred me. No body existed less for me: none existed more. (From the English edition, trans. Patrick O'Brien 19)

Interestingly, Jardine's version of the passage, based on her own translation, also shows omissions as well as changes due to different translations:

> her strained belly, creased in minuscule wrinkles, shriveled, and her shaved pubis [. . .] Seeing my mother's sex organs (*voir le sexe de ma mère*): that gave me quite a shock. No body existed less for me— nor existed more. (qtd. in Jardine 94)

In Jardine's quotation the dialogue between Beauvoir and her mother is deleted. By deleting the dialogue and the introduction to the incident from her mother's perspective ("Maman had an open nightdress on and she did not mind that her wrinkled belly. . .), Jardine specifically foregrounds the body of Beauvoir's mother. She also chooses the more literal translation of *"voir le sexe de ma mère."* "Seeing my mother's sex organs" is far more stark than Patrick O'Brien's translation (done for the 1965 English edition): "The sight of my mother's nakedness . . ." (19). Jardine demonstrates that Beauvoir exposes her mother's body in words in order "to evacuate the dangerous body, the poisoned body, so that she [Beauvoir] may continue to write" (94) but then revalorizes her mother as phallic when she dreams, lying next to her mother in bed, that her mother has become Sartre. Though Jardine's points are well taken, she makes her points by looking at the text from a precise angle.

In short, Jardine focuses on Beauvoir's descriptions of her mother's body while the Cahill anthology deletes the body in order to present a positive mother-daughter relationship. The opposing pivots of Cahill and Jardine's readings parallel the critical response to the text. The body of the text—literally Beauvoir's mother's body—becomes the site of critical blindness and/or insight. The body is either seen or absent and the text has been variously called a masterpiece, indelicate, honest, moving, beautiful, and brutal.

A Very Easy Death arouses controversy because it is textually irritating. It is neither a touching memorial or a caustic dissection of her mother's body. Yet the intersection of clinical discourse and emotional asides—a clash of logos and pathos—makes a reader uneasy. The book treads on sacred ground. A mother's body, particularly a mother's dying body, may be eulogized or sentimentalized, but certainly not made sexually explicit. When Beauvoir refers to her mother's bald pubis—her sex organs—she breaks taboos.

In "Stabat Mater," Julia Kristeva traces the taboos surrounding the mother's body back to the Virgin Mary: the original mother in Western culture. From the Virgin Mary comes the idealization of the mother and the concept of the "virginal maternal." Because the mother has been spiritualized, she is also desexualized and her body parts become prey to cultural regulation: "Of the virginal body we are entitled only to the ear, the tears and the breasts" (Kristeva 108). The mother's breasts, symbolizing nurturance and the mother/child bond, are culturally transformed from sexual to sacred objects and may thus be revealed; the rest of the body (particularly the vagina) is under erasure: "The virgin mother's ample blue gown will allow only the breast to be seen of the body underneath . . ." (109).

The mother's pubis, the site of sexuality, is thus veiled, hidden from public gaze in the same manner as death is hidden by the screens Beauvoir describes being used in the hospital's public wards. In both cases, for the mother or the dying patient, the privacy ordained is designed for the protection of the spectator, who does not want to see. Beauvoir, also, turns away from the sight of her mother's bald pubis, but then in writing about it looks again and forces us to look as well. Laurie Corbin, in *The Mother Mirror: Self-Representation and the Mother-Daughter Relation in College, Simone de Beauvoir, and Marguerite Duras* (1996), also comments on the "violence" of Beauvoir's "discomfort" (53) and credits her shock to the "series of oppositions" produced by the sight: "the presence or absence of the maternal body are contrasted, love is opposed to repulsion, the sacred and repellent nature of the taboo is noted" (53). In short, the sight catches Beauvoir by surprise and forces her to confront all her ambivalence about the maternal body in general and her mother's body in particular. Further, her mother's sexual organs, doubly exposed by the gaping nightdress and by being shaved, become even more shocking within the context of disease and death.

Beauvoir's first reaction to the sight of her mother's sex organs is to turn away. By Freudian theorization, her reaction is male. Accordingly, Lynne Joyrich theorizes that in Freudian terms, the vagina is an "uncanny" sight for men, evoking castration anxiety and "the fear associated with the return to an intrauterine existence . . ." (14). Further, Joyrich speculates "the maternal female body, once home to us all, is the ultimate site of repression" (15). It is—to be sure—a more prosaic site of origin than other modes of birth, e.g., springing full-blown from the head of Zeus. Yet, the reference to Athene's birth is not entirely whimsical; in reading many autobiographers—men or women—one would think many had sprung fully-grown from their father's head, bypassing the need for birth, infancy, and a mother. Jean-Paul Sartre, in his autobiography, *The Words*, makes fun of the tendency of biographers and autobiographers to represent children as "little adults" already demonstrating the traits of the famous writer, inventor, or philosopher, that they would become (203). Conversely, the body of the mother, specifically the mother's vagina, underscores our helplessness, reminding us that we did not spring into the world as little gods. Birth—like death—serves as the great leveler; in dying as in birth, we are all equal and all alone.

When Beauvoir "sees" her mother, the site of origin, she also realizes she is seeing the end, for it is only in the extremities of death that her mother would cease being ashamed of her body. For her whole life Beauvoir's mother had worked to avoid her own flesh; Beauvoir remembers that "Both for her daughters and for herself, she pushed the contempt for the body to the point of uncleanliness" (37). In another autobiographical text, Nancy Friday similarly describes the persona of asexuality mothers impose on themselves to safeguard their sexless image and their daughter's virginity:

> By trying to protect her daughter from sexual hazards which, imagined or not, lie far in the future, the mother begins, from the daughter's birth, to withhold the model of herself as a woman who takes pleasure and pride in sexuality. The daughter is deprived of the identification she needs most. Every effort on the daughter's part to feel good about herself as a woman will be an uphill struggle—if not betrayal—against this sexless image of her mother. (22)

This time, however, in opposition to her portrayal of her mother in *Memoirs of a Dutiful Daughter*, Beauvoir attempts to reconstruct her mother's history, re-visioning her mother as a daughter, so that her mother may be understood as victim as well as perpetrator.

Importantly, Beauvoir does not withhold the unpleasant. She still finds her mother somewhat stupid, often silly, and similarly refuses to idealize her disease—her mother's cancer is described in relentless, clinical detail. When her mother, for example, is unable to control her bowels until the nurse arrives with the bedpan, Beauvoir tries to comfort her. Her mother's reply is chillingly ironic: "Yes . . . the dead certainly do it in their beds" (54). But Beauvoir admires her mother's rejection of her former "proud sensitivities" (54) as well as her indomitable will to live and, repeatedly surprised at her own depth of emotion, finally asks herself: "Why did my mother's death shake me so deeply?" (102).

Beyond the obvious answer—that this was her mother however much Beauvoir previously tried to efface her textually and/or literally—Beauvoir finds in her mother's death that she has been forced to confront her own body and mortality, a confrontation at odds with her typically anti-essentialist stance. Accordingly, as she makes the funeral arrangements with Poupette, after their mother has died, Beauvoir thinks: "We were taking part in the dress rehearsal for our own burial" (100). And Beauvoir perceives, also, that there is nothing "spiritual" about death; illness and disease hideously foreground the body, grotesquely mocking the empty mastery of mind and intellect.

What Beauvoir starts in *A Very Easy Death* she does not finish. The complex representation of her mother gets somewhat cast aside at the end of the book when Beauvoir retreats into general comments about death. Yet, without sentiment, Beauvoir attempts to really see her mother, and in seeing her, sees herself. Beauvoir is also forced, in caring for her mother, to radically shift perspectives. As opposed to the more gradual course Kathleen Woodward outlines, where a woman is first "daughter to her mother," then "mother to her daughter," and finally, "as she grows older . . . becomes mother to her mother" ("Aging" 96), Beauvoir, childless, switches directly from a daughter to her mother to the mother of her mother. Perhaps it is this compression of events that creates the intense focus of *A Very Easy Death*. Moreover, in this text Beauvoir crafts an autobiographical work where the portrayal of the daughter is not accomplished by simplifying and/or effacing the mother. Instead, Beauvoir's stark representation of her mother exceeds generic expectations, frays accepted cultural margins, and calls into question what may, can, and should be written about mothers.

III

The Mother as Spectacle: Erotic Surfaces

What seduces is . . . the fact that it is directed at you. It is seductive to be seduced, and consequently, it is being seduced that is seductive. In other words, the being seduced finds himself in the person seducing. What the person seduced sees in the one who seduces him, the unique object of his fascination, is his own seductive, charming self, his lovable self-image . . .

— Jean Baudrillard, *Seduction*

I gaze at her fine, pink face, glowing in the window light. Her dark hair has small, tight, tight, tight waves. They glow in the light. Everything glows. I am aglow with the rapture of the revelation that she is the most beautiful in the whole world, my mother . . . . It is an intensely aesthetic pleasure . . .

— Adele Wiseman, *Old Woman at Play*

Mothers, Daughters, and Desire

If Simone de Beauvoir worried about becoming "like" mothers and her own mother in particular, my daughter took the notion of transformation one step further. During a conversation about "growing up," Elizabeth, four years old and not yet matrophobic, asked me when her name was going to change to mine. She decided, evidently, that a daughter would not only become *like* a mother but would, in fact, become/replace the mother. Elizabeth's perception, no matter how befuddled, demonstrates her knowledge of gender—she will not become her father—as well as her intuition regarding her future. Clearly, Elizabeth perceived me as a mirror, echoing the commentary of Kathleen Woodward (who uses Doris Bernstein's theory of female identity as her base):

> Thus we could say that (these are not Bernstein's terms) the female
> infant is a mirror for the mother just as the mother is a mirror for the
> little girl. With the mother and the infant girl facing each other, it is
> as if we have the fascinating phenomenon of two mirrors facing each
> other, reflecting each other's surfaces . . . (97)

In short, part of what typifies the mother-daughter relation is this reciprocal and narcissistic gaze. Although the gaze mothers and daughters
share could be termed erotic—the pleasure elicited borders on sexual desire—it is arguable whether it mimes the dynamics of the male gaze. E.
Ann Kaplan posits that the mother-child gaze is "mutual," unlike the
gaze men direct at women that is "the subject-object kind that reduces
one of the parties to the place of submission" (324). But the notion of
"mutual" gazing between mothers and children suggests an uncompli-
cated symbiosis that may simplify the complex desires at work between
mother and daughter. Further, mutuality implies a balance that effaces
the ego and one's ability to initiate desire. Accordingly, Kaplan argues
that women—traditionally—do not "actively" desire but learn to react to
the desire of others (men):

> In the symbolic world the girl now enters she learns not only sub-
> ject/object positions but the sexed pronouns "he" and "she." As-
> signed to the place of object (since she lacks the phallus, the symbol
> of the signifier), she is the recipient of male desire, the passive recipi-
> ent of his gaze. If she is to have sexual pleasure, it can only be con-
> structed around her objectification; it cannot be a pleasure that comes
> from desire for the other (a subject position)—that is *her desire is to
> be desired.* (emphasis added, 316)

Textually, then, a woman would only be able to experience desire if she
were given the script of someone else's desire to read in advance. Simone de Beauvoir says as much in an interview when she describes the
dynamics of her own erotic desire: "In fact, I never desired any man
unless he desired me, too. It was always the other person's desire for me

that swept me away" (qtd. in Schwarzer 112). The woman as a passive recipient of desire echoes, of course, the standard Freudian explanation of male versus female desire. As Jessica Benjamin points out, though, according to Freudian theory, before the daughter is co-opted by the father's gaze, she does go through a period of active desire: "She loves her mother actively until she discovers, in the Oedipal phase, that she and mother both lack the phallus. She becomes feminine only when she turns from the mother to her father " (87). Though the love/desire/gaze between the mother and daughter may be reciprocal, it is questionable whether it is ever *equal* and may, in fact, be just as prone to the play of power and domination equated with the male gaze.

Certainly one could argue that the desire between mothers and daughters might be considered a bit more innocent—or at least not really erotic. The division this argument implies between innocent desire and erotic desire is interesting. Unquestionably, desire can be both; a child's fascination with his/her own body, for example, is at once erotic and innocent. Also, and at the same time, desire is always connected to fluctuations of power. Is desire, then, ever *completely* "innocent," i.e., "artless" or "free from knowledge"?

Accordingly, power is certainly set into motion for mothers who gaze at their child narcissistically to find their "self in the child . . . as an extension of their own egos" (Kaplan 323). And, in a parallel fashion, the daughter who appropriates her mother's body to play out her own hungers and desires transforms mutual gazing into the "subject-object kind" Kaplan sees typifying the male gaze. That the daughter would focus so intensely on the mother's body may be inherent; from birth, the mother sets the child's desire in motion and as demonstrated in the previous chapter, the mother is structured by society to be seen as body. Further, if the mother is viewed as a distant mirror, the mother's beauty may predict the daughter's beauty and—though the connection between beauty and sexuality generally remains unspoken—the daughter knows her beauty implicitly corresponds to her ability to be perceived as a seductive body. Similarly, Carol Ascher looks at her mother (clad only in her underwear) and—in somewhat self-interested terms—identifies her mother's body as an agreeable forecast: "I look over at her in her bra and panties as I pull off my own sweater and slacks. I am surprised by her youthful body. Although she is not slim, her flesh has remained round and buoyant. I feel pleased, more secure about how my own body will look in thirty years" (177). Clearly, her mother's body triggers Ascher's pleasure because it suggests her own body will remain "youthful," "round," "buoyant," and thus desirable.

In extremely misogynist but not culturally off-target terms, Georges Bataille theorizes on the conjunction between beauty and eroticism. According to Bataille, the ideal erotic female is young and beautiful to the degree to which her appearance is "removed from the animal" (143). Perversely, her eroticism hinges on both the sense that her "ethereal" beauty denies the animal while at the same time her body "suggests her private parts, the hairy ones, to be precise" (143). Since Bataille already links beauty and youth with eroticism, his correlative comes as no surprise. Rather bluntly, he states "For a man, there is nothing more depressing than an ugly woman, for then the ugliness of the organs and the sexual act cannot show up in contrast" (145). Consequently, while a daughter is unlikely to dwell on her own beauty and/or sexuality she may present her mother's body and, by indirection, suggest her own. Perhaps most important, then, is the fact that the mother provides a "safe" body for the daughter. If, as Shirley Neuman has posited, "Bodies rarely figure in autobiography" (1), a daughter may displace her corporeal desires, hungers, and dissatisfactions onto the body of her mother without risking the exposure of her own body. In classic psychoanalysis (and—apparently—in women's autobiography) "motherhood is ultimately the child's drama" while the mother serves as the "essential but silent Other, the mirror in whom the child searches for [her] own reflection, the body [she] seeks to appropriate" (Suleiman 357). By focusing on her mother's physical appearance rather than her own, a daughter may stay securely within autobiography's spiritual/cultural trajectory while transposing her desires onto her mother's body.

Nathalie Sarraute's *Childhood*: The Mother as Lack

> But besides these minute separate details, how did I first become con-
> scious of what was always there—her astonishing beauty? Perhaps I
> never became conscious of it; I think I accepted her beauty as the
> natural quality that a mother—she seemed typical, universal, yet our
> own in particular—had by virtue of being our mother. It was part of
> her calling. I do not think that I separated her face from that general
> being; or from her whole body.
>
> —Virginia Woolf, *Moments of Being*

In Beauvoir's early autobiography, *Memoirs of a Dutiful Daughter*, it is
clear that the mother, for Beauvoir as well as many other autobiographers
as daughters, is relegated to the domestic/bodily/dutiful sphere. In the
Memoirs, the mother tends to Beauvoir's body and guides her moral development. For Beauvoir, her mother is primarily a desexualized, docile
body. But a daughter's interest in her mother's body may also be erotic
as Nathalie Sarraute demonstrates in her autobiography, *Childhood*. In
the autobiography, Sarraute writes a dreamlike account of her childhood
memories and feelings. Though Sarraute's autobiography is set in
Europe (Russia, France, and Switzerland) in the early 1900s, her autobiography—like Beauvoir's—contains few references to time and place.
Sarraute uses an evocative narrative style permeating the text with visual,
aural, gustatory, and tactile images that unfold across the autobiography's sensual landscape.

The narrative technique of the autobiography is initially confusing.
Two voices—both apparently originating from the narrator's consciousness—carry on a dialogue. In the original French version of *Childhood*,
these two voices make the crisscrossing paths of allegory and irony particularly evident. Repeatedly, Sarraute highlights childhood moments
where she tests limits, margins, or commits minor transgressive acts.
The bulk of those highlighted, spatialized fragments are written in the
feminine gender (a distinction evident in the French language, not in

English) while a second voice, of masculine gender, critiques, analyzes, and "comments on the incompleteness and possible falsifications of the dominant voice of feminine gender" (O'Callaghan 84). In short, the trajectory of allegory is presented by an affective, fluid feminine voice while the masculine voice, probing and unfolding the moments the feminine voice has elicited, discloses the vertical movement of irony.

Within Sarraute's impressionistic autobiography, the characterizations—aside from that of her mother, father, stepmother, half-sister—are blurred and inconsequential. Of the few characters that are foregrounded, by far the most enigmatic and interesting character Sarraute presents is that of her mother. Sarraute's troubled and ambivalent relationship with her mother may be evidenced by the degree of ironic probing that surrounds each incident she and her mother share; no other character provokes as much commentary by the masculine ironic voice as that of her mother. Further, the masculine/feminine voices in some ways replicate the tension between masculine and feminine, mother and father that Sarraute experiences in childhood. Raylene L. Ramsey (formerly Raylene O'Callaghan), in *The French New Autobiographies: Sarraute, Duras, and Robbe-Grillet* (1996), explains how the "masculine and feminine voices" help dramatize the strain Sarraute feels "as she is pulled in opposite directions by loyalties to divorced parents"; here again, the association of the mother with body and emotion and the father with intellect may be observed:

> The charming silken, adored mother demands absolute loyalty and devotion from her daughter but a number of the scenes that portray her are implicitly critical. The calmer sketches of the sternly moral, more cerebral, reserved, but loving and silently complicitous father, curiously the only presence at the child's bedside during a severe reaction to a diphtheria inoculation, also appear to be part of the writer's attempt to understand the sentiments of those close to her . . . (57)

Yet, despite the interplay of voices and the careful probing of each incident, Sarraute never seems to come any closer to understanding her parents and—in particular—her baffling mother.

Like Beauvoir's mother, Sarraute's mother is beautiful. Though the beauty of Beauvoir's mother seems almost incidental or expected, the beauty of Sarraute's mother is explicitly foregrounded: she is an erotic body. Consistently, in the autobiographies where the mother is credited with exerting the least cultural or intellectual impact, the mother's image is often the most beautiful. But why must the mother be beautiful?

A scene from *Childhood* proves suggestive. Sarraute, walking with her mother, sees a beautiful doll in a shop window. Much to Sarraute's "embarrassment" and "distress," an uncomfortable idea forms in her mind (81). The doll is more beautiful than her mother. Sarraute—even as a child—intuits the magnitude of her betrayal but finally voices it anyhow and tells her mother, "I think she's more beautiful than you" (84). Her mother lets go of Sarraute's hand—disconnecting their bodies—and says "A child who loves its mother thinks that no one is more beautiful than she" (84).

The scene serves to suggest a number of reasons for the preponderance of beautiful mothers in women's autobiographies. If the mother has been reduced to body, a terrain for the daughter to explore and use as a mirror for her own maturation, the mother's claim to difference/différance (love rests on singularity) depends on her physicality. Sarraute previously does not question her mother's beauty, considering it "far removed from all possible comparison" (82). By judging her mother, Sarraute removes her mother from the position of unquestioned adoration and puts her in the category of "others" where "people compare, situate, assign places . . ." (85). Textually, the body of the mother would then no longer function as a unique signifier. Sarraute's mother, perceiving her own erasure, uses guilt as retaliation: you don't love me.

In Sarraute's example, numerous shifts in power and desire between the mother and daughter may be seen in the incident's underlying dynamics. If Sarraute's mother is worshipped as body, a uniquely beautiful map for the daughter to survey and adore, her mother's love for Sarraute rests upon her ability to conform: a good daughter loves her mother without question. This is what Sarraute's mother means when she says, "A child who loves its mother thinks that no one is more beautiful than she" (84). Importantly, in her mother's rebuke, Sarraute is not called by her name or even identified by a personal pronoun, but instead relegated to the general category of childhood.

Conversely, when Sarraute questioned her mother's beauty, she displaced her mother from a position that was unique and unquestioned to a position where she could be compared and assessed "among the others" (85). Sarraute's mother re-asserts her power by reminding Nathalie that as a child she is part of a general category with clearly defined guidelines. A child loves her mother, and, because of this love "thinks her more beautiful than anyone else in the world" (85). Accordingly, if Nathalie does not "love" her mother (she transfers her desire to the hairdresser's doll) she is abnormal, aberrant, and without signification, as Sarraute indicates when she questions herself: "What child doesn't love her [mother]? Where has that ever been known? Nowhere. It wouldn't be a child, it would be a monster" (85).

Throughout the incident Sarraute describes concerning her mother and the doll, Nathalie plays, somewhat perversely, with the idea of disappearance and reconstitution. She knows her comment about the doll may create a schism between herself and her mother but makes the comment anyhow. When her mother retaliates, Sarraute toys with the idea of her own disappearance by seeing herself as an aberrant child that existed "nowhere." Sarraute's desire for presence, although she continually describes and orchestrates scenes of absence, surfaces throughout her autobiography. Significantly, the body of Sarraute's mother becomes the critical site of lack and the recurrent absence of her mother's body initiates the atmosphere of hunger and desire that pervades the autobiography.

When Sarraute writes of her mother she talks in terms of proximity—how close her mother's body is to hers, whether her mother is leaving or trying to leave, how her mother's body looks and feels, the warmth of her mother's leg, the silkiness of her skin, the softness of her hair. Sarraute's descriptions of her mother are lush, detailed, and heavy with unfulfilled desire:

> I loved her fine, delicate features, as if they were blended . . . . I can't find any other word . . . with her golden, rosy skin, soft and silky to the touch, more silky than silk, warmer and more tender than the feathers of a baby bird, than its down . . . . Her gaze was rather strange . . . often as if *absent.* (82 emphasis added)

Though Sarraute repeatedly associates her mother's expressions and demeanor with distance and absence, and comments that her mother "really did have that kind of absence which occasionally made her inaccessible to everyone" (83), it is clear that her mother is most absent to Nathalie. If Sarraute cannot achieve real *presence* by breaking through her mother's veneer of preoccupation and indifference, she can verbally appropriate her mother's surface—her body—by reproducing it, in sensuous detail, into text.

Sarraute's textualization of her mother's body—though motivated by different circumstances—parallels in some ways the mind/body, father/mother split enacted by Beauvoir. Sarraute's father, like Beauvoir's, represents intellect, common sense, and stability. Raylene O'Callaghan conjectures that the text's masculine voice, that refuses the "self-indulgence" of the feminine voice, represents the "intellectual austerity of the father" (90). In contrast, Sarraute describes her mother as "insouciant," "frivolous" (11), having a gaze of childlike naiveté and writing stories for children in a large, childlike scrawl. Thus, though her mother writes, and would appear to be connected with "logos," Sarraute infantilizes the project. Sarraute has a considerable amount at stake by portraying her mother as somewhat childish, irrational, whimsical—a person who would carelessly arrive or abruptly leave. Repeatedly, Sarraute's mother leaves, and finally, when Nathalie is eight years old, she leaves for good. In short, Sarraute denies her mother any connection with logos because it would rationalize the behavior of a mother who leaves, a mother who does not love her daughter enough to stay. Though, by leaving, Sarraute's mother withdraws her body—paradoxically—her mother's body is all Sarraute has left.

When Sarraute's mother leaves, all that her mother and Sarraute share are surfaces, the images they have constructed of each other. Accordingly, for years Sarraute's mother persists in sending postcards to the eight-year-old girl whose image is frozen in her mind. As Sarraute reads the postcards, she remarks:

> To whom are they addressed, then, the postcards, the letters that Mama sends me? To whom does she think she is telling, as you tell a little child, that, in the place where she and Koyla are having a month's holiday, the little girls wear red ribbons and pretty wooden clogs. She doesn't know who I am now, she has even forgotten who I was. (111)

Importantly, Sarraute caps her observations about her mother's letters by terming their content "*childish* accounts" (emphasis added, 111). By refusing to grant her mother full adult status, Sarraute lessens the pain her mother inflicts by viewing her actions as unpremeditated, as irrational.

Though much of Sarraute's autobiography concerns the impact of language, no one's words affect Sarraute more deeply than her mother's. Like her mother's body, that Sarraute memorizes and dwells on in her absence, her mother's words become solid entities that Sarraute hears, feels, sees, and thinks about long after her mother has left. Sarraute's concretization of her mother's language may be observed, for example, in an instance when she refers to some words her mother has spoken as a "*parcel* she gave to take with her [Sarraute], like the ones you give your child when you are sending it to boarding school" (emphasis added 167). Her mother's language becomes, in fact, *body*; her words literally embodied by Sarraute who perceives her mother's language as a hypnotic, invasive force: "Yes, curiously enough that indifference, that casualness, were part of her [her mother's] charm, in the literal sense of the word, she charmed me . . . . No word, however peacefully uttered, has ever sunk into me with the same percussive force as some of hers" (19).

And yet these words, that may—in a phallic gesture—puncture Sarraute's body, operate on a pre-symbolic register; her mother's language is "charming" but irrational. Sarraute continually finds out, after investigation, that her mother's words make no sense. She does not need to chew her food "until it has become *as* liquid as soup" (8), she does not "die" when she touches an electrical pole (19), and she did not grow in her mother's stomach because her mother had "eaten some dust" (21).

Her mother's words, however, take on critical mass because of their rarity. Like her mother's body, Sarraute can never get enough of it/them. For Sarraute, her mother's language, like her mother's body, demonstrates the perverse dynamics of desire: "Desire has the contradictory nature by being that which exceeds the bounds of the imaginary satisfaction available to the demand" (Gallop 13). Since neither Sarraute's hunger for her mother's body or her mother's words can ever be satisfied, the two—body and language—become the same in Sarraute's mind. Sarraute's textual conflation of her mother's words and body may be evidenced as she quickly shifts from describing her desire for her mother's words to her desire for her mother's body:

> One affectionate word from Mama was enough, or even just seeing her, sitting in her armchair reading, raising her head, looking surprised when I go up and speak to her, she looks at me . . . and I cuddle up to her, I put my lips on the delicate, silky, soft skin of her forehead, of her cheeks. (31)

Sarraute's mother performs similar displacements of word and body. When Sarraute suggests calling her stepmother, "Mama-Vera," her mother is outraged. In her body's absence, her mother realizes the signifier *mama* acts as a substitute and maintains her privileged position in relation to Nathalie. Narcissistically, Sarraute's mother desires

Nathalie's unequivocal devotion; linking her name with that of another [mother] would put her unique position as mother under erasure: "This name of Mama cannot be coupled to any other . . . [mother is] a name that can be given to no other woman . . ." (194).

Not surprisingly, when Sarraute's mother visits—after a four-year absence—they assess each other in terms of their bodies, their surfaces. They stand facing each other, weighing and mirroring each other's desires. Like Beauvoir, Sarraute's reaction to her mother is riddled with ambivalence: "no body existed less for me: none existed more" (Beauvoir 1964, 19). Sarraute first notes her mother has put on some weight and has a hair style that makes her look a "little commonplace, a little hard" (222), but then succumbs nonetheless to her mother's charm, her mother's body: "But as soon as my lips touch her skin . . . I know no other skin like it, softer and silkier than everything soft and silky in the world . . . . I want to stretch out my hand once again and caress her hair" (223).

Conversely, as Sarraute reads her mother's face, trying to assess her mother's desire for her, she feels she has disappointed her mother, that her body is no longer "pretty enough to eat" (223). As they continue to look at each other, their inability to do more than merely mirror each other's desire, to reflect each other's surface, paralyzes them. They literally cannot speak: "We stay there facing each other, we look at each other, I don't know what to say, and I can see that Mama doesn't really know what to say either" (224).

Sarraute and her mother do not know what to say to each other because their relationship no longer operates on a symbolic, verbal level. Each has been reduced to body by the other's desire. Hopelessly, Sarraute keeps trying to reconstitute the mother that was never really there in the first place. Sarraute focuses all the physical intimacy she has not received from her father, stepmother, and particularly from her own mother, onto her mother's body. Yet, however much Nathalie's mother exerts her power, Sarraute, in writing about her mother and—in particular—her mother's body, has the "last word." Textually, Sarraute has the upper hand since, as Laurie Corbin explains, the daughter ultimately "writes" the mother:

> The mother in these texts [autobiographies] can only reflect the daughter's imposition of her own view. In other words, if a mother's face appears in the mirror, it is the daughter's vision of herself which put it there. The concept of the mother as mirror will always relegate the mother to the position of object, rather than subject. (144)

This shift in power, however, only comes later, when Sarraute actually writes the autobiography. At the time of the actual auotbiographical events, Sarraute's mother carefully scripts the way she wants Nathalie to interpret her. Accordingly, Sarraute's mother will not yield her position as mother; her desire is to be desired. In a sense, according to Freudian formulation, Sarraute's desire is the more active while her mother's is passive. Their desire for each other mimics, therefore, the dynamics of male-female desire—the "subject-object kind"—that E. Anne Kaplan saw generated by the male gaze. Sarraute's desire, predicated on lack (the absent mother), is active, creative and, psychoanalytically speaking, male. Her mother's desire, dependent on the desire Nathalie displays for her, is passive and female.

Whether desire can be so neatly gendered remains questionable. Clearly, desire is riddled with power and ambiguity whether its genesis is male or female, from a child or adult. It is, however, apparent that the lack generated by an absent mother can create a subject-object dynamics of desire that reduces both the mother and daughter to the sight/site of body. Similarly, as may be seen in the autobiographies of Maya Angelou, Mary McCarthy, or Charlotte Perkins Gilman, the mother's absence—metaphorical or literal—creates an emotional void for the daughter who displaces her affections onto the mother's (actual or remembered) body. Conversely, for Beauvoir, who—like Irigaray—chokes on her mother's ever-presence, the dynamics is reversed; the mother is not desired but still reduced to body as her physicality becomes the object of the daughter's rejection and fear. Nancy Mairs offers an insightful explanation of how a mother is somewhat thrust into the role of squelching desire and thus becoming a figure of oppression:

> . . . she [Mair's mother] was only exhibiting that reflexive maternal guilt which emerges at the infant's first wail: "I'm sorry. I'm sorry. I'm sorry I pushed you from this warm womb into the arms of strangers, me among them. I'm sorry I can't keep you perfectly full, perfectly dry, perfectly free from gas and fear, perfectly, perfectly happy." Any mother knows that if she could do these things, her infant would die more surely than if she covered its face with a rose-printed pillow. *Still, part of her desire is to prevent the replication of desire.* ("Plaintext" emphasis added, 75)

The mother a daughter views as oppressive becomes a body to be repelled since she threatens to invade the daughter's own bodily margins and to destroy the daughter's own desires. Either way, however, whether the daughter perceives the mother as lack or excess, the equation remains the same: mother equals body.

Annie Dillard's *An American Childhood*
Mothers, Daughters, and Bodies:
Culturally Trapped, Beautifully Wrapped

> I saw my mother's own menstrual blood before I saw my own. Hers was the first female body I ever looked at, to know what women were, what I was to be . . . . As a young child I thought how beautiful she was; a print of Botticelli's Venus on the wall, half-smiling, hair flowing, associated itself in my mind with her. In early adolescence I still glanced slyly at my mother's body, vaguely imagining: I too shall have breasts, full hips, hair between my thighs—whatever that meant to me then, and with all the ambivalence of such a thought.
>
> —Adrienne Rich, *Of Woman Born*

Annie Dillard's autobiography, *An American Childhood* (1989), though quite recent, conforms remarkably well to the classic traditions of the genre. Echoing Georges Gusdorf's precept that autobiographers write because they believe in their centrality and worth, throughout her autobiography Dillard universalizes her experiences. As Sidonie Smith similarly notes in *Subjectivity, Identity, and the Body* (1993), Dillard's title itself (*An American Childhood*) immediately positions Dillard as a representative figure whose experiences typify American childhood. Smith critiques Dillard's tendency to efface other experience by presenting her own as prototypical:

> Dillard participates in the politics and poetics of exclusion . . . . Dillard represses the figures of difference that have erupted throughout her text. Specific bodies lose their heterogeneous marks of difference. Dillard is not impervious to the shadowy border areas of class and race that push against the edges of her comfortable skin . . . yet in the end she effectively whitewashes identity through her memorial pageant. (138–39)

While Smith constructs a cogent argument, perhaps Dillard's primary focus was less on making her particular, rather privileged socioeconomic life representational than on depicting the experience of childhood itself in terms of its gradual awakening and emerging consciousness. Even so, the world Dillard awakens to, Smith posits, is one of privilege where it is presumed that "the world wants their touch, [and that] the world will touch back" ("Subjectivity" 139).

Ostensibly, in more recent autobiographies, the mother is represented with increased complexity, i.e., as more than a body. Accordingly, Annie Dillard, in *An American Childhood*, describes her mother's humor, quick intelligence, and love of language. Nevertheless, over and over again, Dillard dwells on her mother's body. Similarly, my own daughter, four years old, walked into my bedroom while I was dressing, looked at me, and said that she was going to be a "mess" when she grew up. I understood what she meant. Her statement was literal. My breasts, my body—though small and trim—exceeded the taut margins of a child's contours and filled her with a vague foreboding. There is a similar mix of curiosity and premonition as Annie Dillard describes the body of her mother.

The mother's body provides a dubious forecast for the daughter: she may, perhaps, eventually resemble her mother (which, depending on the daughter's viewpoint, could be good or bad) but she will definitely—like her mother—become older. While Sarraute's depiction of her mother as beautiful underscores Sarraute's own unfulfilled desire and her mother's need to be desired, there are other reasons for a daughter to wish for a beautiful mother.

By representing the mother as beautiful, the daughter may also experience some displaced narcissism. Though a woman writing her autobiography no longer believes, as my daughter did, that she will become her mother, a daughter always is and is not her mother. Luce Irigaray comments similarly on the blurring of mother/daughter boundaries: "You look at yourself in the mirror. And your mother is already there. And soon your daughter [as] mother. Between the two where are you? . . . just a scansion, the time when the one becomes the other" (qtd in Gallop 116).

Shirley Abbott's representation of her mother in *Womenfolks: Growing Up Down South*, enacts Irigaray's point literally and metaphorically. Abbott describes how as a child she would watch her mother methodically apply her make-up. Though Abbott looks into the mirror in her mother's bedroom, it is her mother's face she sees reflected. Sometimes, when her mother had "brought her face to its state of daytime perfection" (16), her mother would take her to town with her. Abbott's close connection to her mother's cosmetic ritual—she opens her mother's jars of creams, offers her advice, and watches her changing face—makes her complicit in her mother's transformation. When Abbott writes, then, that her mother "seemed so beautiful to me in those moments that I loved her with all my heart—indeed I was in love with her" (16), her love—in part reflexive and narcissistic—also extends to herself.

The last time Abbott watches her mother's face reflected in her mirror, she is thirty-three and her mother has cancer. This time, although Abbott again helps her mother with the jars and containers, her mother is unable to make up her face. The dresser drawer, filled with cosmetics, is never opened again and Abbott realizes her mother is dying.

If the mother's image from the vantage of childhood often pleasantly predicts the daughter's own maturation, the adult daughter's image of the aging and/or dying mother brings other emotions. The daughter as autobiographer, generally older than the mother she remembers as a child, is now concerned with her own aging. Her affiliation with her elderly mother prompts what Kathleen Woodward terms a "reactivation of the Oedipus complex" where the identification with the parents, if not as "disagreeable" as Woodward suggests, does elicit ambivalence (1991, 53).

Besides the more predictable emotions of love, sorrow, grief, guilt, denial, and fear that the representation of an elderly or dying parent can incur, the daughter's tendency to focus on the old age of her mother—to describe her physical transformations in detail—also suggests the daughter's perverse desire to dwell on and to literally rehearse her own aging and death (a desire Beauvoir similarly demonstrates in *A Very Easy Death*). In many women's autobiographies, following the descriptions of the mother's aging or death, the daughter provides a final image or reference to her young mother, a gesture providing the daughter power to control the mother's image in language if not in reality.

Similarly, in an essay by Mary Jane Moffat entitled "Giving My Mother a Bath" excerpted from her book, *City of Roses: Stories from Childhood*, Moffat writes a moving account of her mother's aging body. As Moffat bathes her mother (who is recovering from a hip replacement), her mother's seventy-eight year-old body becomes an evocative map that Moffat traces body part by body part while reflecting on her mother's history, her own history, and her own body. Moffat starts by washing her mother's face and then working downward, reading each feature of her mother's body as a predictive and historical text. A lump on her mother's lower lip recalls a car accident; the knotted muscles on her mother's neck reminds Moffat that she and her mother "tighten up in all the same places"; her mother's ample breasts make Moffat reflect on her own breasts and remember how her father once termed them "little walnuts" (94, 96). Moffat hands her mother the washcloth so that she can wash her "privates." Though Moffat "stares at the ceiling during this process," Moffat seems more aware of the moment's symbolic significance than Beauvoir was (in a similar scene in *A Very Easy Death*) and comments how her mother "obediently washes the mysterious and unspeakable regions from which I sprang" (97). When Moffat resumes bathing her mother she again provides a detailed anatomical analysis along with the associations each feature evokes. As Moffat struggles to help her mother out of the tub, her mother finally exclaims angrily, "How did I get so old?" (101). While ostensibly thinking of what to do, Moffat instead—in a redemptive gesture—describes how she used to watch her mother bathe when she was a child and her mother was still young:

> I used to sit on the toilet lid to be near her while she bathed before going to work. She was thin then. Her full breasts rode high above the water line. Her lovely lopsided grin revealed her own teeth. When she kissed me goodbye, she smelled of Blue Grass, not the faint, dank vapors of age. (101)

Although Moffat remains poignantly aware of her mother's fragile mortality, restoring on her mother's youth allows her control; in text if not in reality, Moffat can focus instead on a time when her mother was "never sick" and "never, ever going to die" (101).

In a chapter from *An American Childhood*, Annie Dillard, though describing the young mother she remembers as a child, weaves images of both youth and aging into her portrayal of her mother. Dillard, intensely scrutinizing her mother's body, notes how her own skin—like the skin of other children—fits tightly on her body. Conversely, her mother's skin—as that of other adults—was "loose . . . all over, except at the wrists and ankles, like rabbits" (24). Dillard experiments with her mother's body, noting how when she pinched the skin on her mother's hand, "the pinch didn't snap back; it lay dead across her knuckle in a yellowish ridge" (24). She notes also how she was able to swing the "relaxed flesh" of her mother's calves "like a baby in a sling" (26). Commenting on her mother's, as well as other adults,' unwillingness to run, Dillard decides "it went with being old, apparently, and having their skin half off" (28). Though Dillard writes this chapter with humor, she comments, ambivalently, that she "would not let this happen" to her. The "this" she refers to is, of course, aging.

When Dillard writes her autobiography, or memoir, as she prefers to call it, she is forty. The mother she depicts in this chapter is nearly a decade younger. Despite her mother's youth, Dillard sees—with a child's clarity—the beginnings of aging on her mother's body. Provocatively, however, Dillard balances her more negative representation of her mother's aging body with an awed description of how her mother effected a "transformation" from "an everyday, tender, nap-creased mother into an exalted and dazzling beauty" (27). Dressed up to go out, her mother's loose skin and signs of aging seemed to disappear and Dillard writes glowingly of her mother's transformation:

> Her blue eyes shone and caught the light, and so did the platinum waves in her hair and the pearls at her ears and throat. She was wearing a black dress. The smooth skin on her breastbone rent my heart, it was so familiar and beloved; the black silk bodice and simple necklace set off its human fineness. (27)

In a rare reference to the present—Dillard describes herself writing on a pine desk—she imagines as the sun begins to set, that she sees her mother coming for her. Significantly, though Dillard is forty and her mother is now in her sixties, it is Dillard's young mother she envisions: "Is it Mother coming for me, to carry me home? Could it be my own young, my own glorious Mother, coming . . . to get me and bring me back? Back to where I last knew all I needed, the way to her two strong arms?" (250). In Dillard's vision, not only does her mother become young again, but Dillard also has been transformed back into a little girl.

Dillard's alternating images of her mother's youth and age enact a virtual *fort/da* (gone/there) of representation. Dillard plays, somewhat perversely, with concepts of age and renewal. Restoring her mother's youth and age bears directly on Dillard's own present age and changing body. If the figure of the mother serves as a displaced mirror for both the daughter of the past as well as the daughter of the present, the transformative nature of the mother's representation provides the autobiographer with power: if the mother's body is capable of change and renewal, so is the daughter's. Through language, the daughter may control the image of her mother and, by extension, that of herself and her own aging body.

Dillard, though, has uses for her mother's body other than as a metaphorical means of controlling aging. Her mother's centrality in the book is clear. In a review of *An American Childhood*, Noel Perrin comments that "though scores of people appear, only two of them are real characters: Annie Dillard herself and, for one wonderful chapter, her mother" (7). After reading Dillard's autobiography, Perrin's comment is justified; no one else other than Dillard herself is described as much as her mother.

Throughout *An American Childhood*, Dillard sets out to demonstrate her mother's non-conformity and uniqueness. A positive representation of a mother places the daughter in a double bind. If the mother's role is typically viewed as passive and domestically versus culturally-bound, presenting the mother as a role model jeopardizes the daughter's own representation. Dillard attempts to elude this trap by demonstrating how her mother exceeds/deviates from the implicit maternal norm. Ostensibly, Dillard attempts to prove how her mother's character and intelligence set her apart from the other mothers, yet over and over again what Dillard returns to, in her descriptions, is her mother's body. Nevertheless, her mother may be admired and emulated if Dillard can prove her mother differs from other mothers. The subtext of this agenda is revealing; if a "good" mother, that is, a mother worthy of emulation, *differs* from all other mothers, what does this say about motherhood?

Early in the book, Dillard describes the confined space allotted for the [other] mothers in the early 1950s: "Every woman stayed alone in her house in those days, like a coin in a safe" (16). Though Dillard's mother clearly functions as one of those coins "in the safe," Dillard's project, in large measure, is to demonstrate how her mother's "specialness" transcends the space of normal maternal confines, e.g., she is more intelligent, more sensitive to social issues, and more eccentric than the "other" mothers. Since Dillard calls into question her mother's individuality, she invites the reader to consider how "role-breaking" her mother really is.

Clearly, her mother is intelligent and articulate. Within the conservative milieu of Pittsburgh's upper middle class in the 1950s, however, she operates like a maelstrom, that is, like a storm with a narrowly confined circumference. For all her mother's intelligence and wit, she makes little headway; all her innovations and ideas whirl harmlessly within culturally accepted boundaries. Her victory over the U.S. Post Office makes a good story to tell over cocktails: "When we moved across town she persuaded the U.S. Post Office to let her keep her old address—forever—because she'd had stationery printed . . . . Every new post office worker, over decades, needed to learn that although the Doaks' mail is addressed to here, it is delivered to there" (115). Power and privilege undercut the story's humor. For all her mother's determination, we know her success is largely accomplished by the family's position within Pittsburgh.

Dillard also notes the paradox and remarks that her "Mother's energy and intelligence suited her for a greater role in a larger arena . . . . She saw how things should be run, but she had nothing to run but her household" (115). Yet, this isn't entirely true. Dillard's mother frequently comments on the bigotry and injustice around her but keeps her involvement at a performative, verbal level. Though she believes, Dillard asserts, that "the country-club pool sweeper was a person, and that the department-store saleslady, the bus driver, telephone operator, and housepainter were people, and even in groups the steelworkers who carried pickets and the Christmas shoppers who clogged intersections were people" (117), there is little evidence in Dillard's autobiography that her mother does much to effect change.

Consistently, her mother's activities conform to that of a married woman within Pittsburgh's Presbyterian elite: she goes to dinners, spends a great deal of time at their country club, decorates and re-decorates their house, runs errands, and works on her tan in the backyard. In truth, she practices a "safe" non-conformity by disrupting the etiquette of bridge games and conversationally noting social injustices.

Even her mother's body implicitly conforms to their culture's affluent standards. Repeatedly, Dillard proudly comments on her mother's beautiful body: slender, youthful, tan, and blond. It becomes clear that it is her mother's beauty, her mother's body that—for Dillard—makes her mother particularly special and unique. She describes, for example, in a scene presented as part of a typical day, how she and her friend, Pin, see their mothers tending to their bodies:

> We came home and found our mothers together in our side yard by the rose garden, tanning on chaise lounges. *They were both thin and blond.* They held silvered cardboard reflectors up to their flung-back chins. Over their closed eyelids they had placed blue eye-shaped plastic cups, joined over the nose. (emphasis added, 125)

Inherent in Dillard's description of the two mothers is how actively they work to make their bodies conform to social standards. Their thinness and tan-ness are part of their lives; correspondingly, Dillard reflects, with some irony, on how a woman at their country club who was "a prominent figure . . . never washed her face all summer, to preserve her tan" (216). In short, these women recognize that their bodies—slim and tan—signal affluence. Susan Bordo similarly critiques the status and elegance that became increasingly associated with slenderness in the twentieth century:

The gracefully slender body announced aristocratic status; disdainful of the bourgeois need to display wealth and power ostentatiously, it commanded social space invisibly rather than aggressively, seemingly above the commerce in appetite or the need to eat. Subsequently, this ideal began to be appropriated by the status-seeking middle class, as slender wives became the showpieces of their husbands' success. (94)

The problem Dillard has with her "positive" representation of her mother, therefore, a problem that occurs in her own representation as she describes her adolescence, cannot be textually resolved. Though Dillard attempts to show her mother as a non-conformist and, in a parallel fashion, tries to present her own non-conformity during adolescence, both Dillard and her mother emerge as docile bodies. Accordingly, when Dillard—in her teens—describes how she breaks with the church in a gesture she herself views as performative, her parents' reactions are telling. Her mother worries how it will reflect on the family and her father's rebuke addresses the "method" rather than content of her religious rebellion: "He went on: But didn't I see? That people did these things—quietly? Just—quietly? No fuss? No flamboyant gestures" (227).

By the standards of her parents and their society, Dillard's adolescence is messy and uncontrolled. When Dillard's sister also enters adolescence, her mother sends her to boarding school rather than "subjecting the family to two adolescent maelstroms whirling at once in the same house" (235). Clearly, Dillard has no more chance of escaping the conforming pressures of her society than her mother did. Unless Dillard would decide to reject her community entirely, she would become, in Foucault's sense of the term, an increasingly docile body: "A body is docile that may be subjected, used, transformed and improved" (136). And, for Dillard, adolescence is a process of docilization. She must be properly improved and "shaped," and, accordingly, Dillard is sent off to Hollins College to "smooth off her rough edges" (243). Significantly, the metaphor of smoothing off "rough edges" refers to sculpting, a visual process reinforcing the concept of woman as body and spectacle rather than mind.

What Samuel Hazo might have been sensing when he wrote that Dillard's "book could have ended on page 150 and finished stronger" (638) is the tension that arises as Dillard describes her adolescence. The first half of the autobiography, dealing with Dillard's childhood and pre-adolescence, does not disappoint. Dillard's project—to capture the consciousness of a child waking up into life—is poignantly realized. When she represents her mother from the perspective a little girl—as in the chapter when she describes her mother's skin—her writing is fresh and unforced.

In part, Dillard's ability to engagingly present her body and mind in early childhood is aided by our own romanticization of children. As Shirley Neuman points out, generally, in autobiographies, only children's bodies are portrayed and "(mis)represented, with Rousseauistic rather than Hollywood idealism, as uninscribed by culture" (1). When Dillard presents herself in adolescence, then, she cannot as easily present the innocent, unrestrained, physical joy of childhood, and, as her earlier excitement and wonder in her world fades, she resembles in many ways the doomed Polyphemous moth she describes in her autobiography. The moth grotesquely outgrows its Mason jar. When it is released into the world, the moth cannot fly but may only crawl endlessly down a "broad black driveway" with "its shriveled wings . . . glued shut" (161).

Emily Hancock, in her 1989 study, *The Girl Within*, similarly explains how many women lose touch with the "self-possessed" child they were before puberty as they become increasingly stunted by cultural expectations:

> As the older girl succumbs to culture's image of the female, her childhood displays give way to hiding—skills, excellence, aspirations, parts of the self—first from others in order to please, eventually also from herself . . . . Female roles impinge; stereotypes take over. A young girl projecting herself into the future can't help but feel

caught by contradictory imperatives: even as she dons her soccer uniform, ads for deodorant implore, "Never let them see you sweat." (22)

The strain Hazo notes in the last half of Dillard's autobiography, then, may arise from the combined stress of audience and genre. Dillard's acquiescence to the conforming drives of society during adolescence undermines her ability to represent herself as autonomous. In part, Dillard's textually confusing adolescence derives from the conflicting goals of her autobiographical project. On the one hand, Dillard attempts to portray herself as representational—i.e., a girl having a typical "American Childhood," and, at the same time, Dillard tries to fashion herself into a "unique" adolescent. Correspondingly, her desire to represent her mother as a non-conformist when there is no evidence of her mother's ability or inclination to break away from cultural expectations also rings false.

Not surprisingly, most autobiographies by women either end with childhood or begin in adulthood. For a woman typically—and certainly within the conservative American (white) upper middle-class culture of the late 1950s Dillard describes—there is nothing particularly autonomous about adolescence. Historically, in adolescence, women learn to become more feminine, subdued, and focused on attracting men. In parallel terms, Hancock depicts a woman's adolescence as a time when a female "loses her self-possession; she loses her sense of self as subject, she senses that she is now 'other' and becomes object in a male world" (22). If autobiography—traditionally—highlights the course of an "unfettered" individual, a woman autobiographer's dilution and/or deletion of her adolescence might be a savvy maneuver.

Dillard is also extremely aware of her audience. Most specifically, she is aware of her mother. As Dillard writes her autobiography, her mother is still alive. Dillard's representation of her mother, judging from what we learn about her in the autobiography, seems very much the portrait her mother would enjoy: that of an intelligent, engagingly eccentric, and beautiful young woman. Dillard's desire to please her mother—as well as the rest of her family—becomes apparent when Dillard writes [albeit ironically], in an article about *An American Childhood*, of the parts in her life she omitted:

> I tried to leave out anything that might trouble my family. My parents are quite young. My sisters are watching this book carefully . . . .I have no temptation to air grievances; in fact, I have no grievances left. Unfortunately, I seem to have written the story of my adolescence so convincingly that my parents (after reading that section of the book) think I still feel that way. It's a problem I have to solve—one of many in this delicate area. My parents and my youngest sister still live in Pittsburgh; I have to handle it with tongs. ("To Fashion a Text" 69)

Similarly, a daughter's need to handle the representation of a living mother "with tongs" may also be evidenced in the (first) autobiography of Maya Angelou, *I Know Why the Caged Bird Sings*. Like Dillard, Angelou writes her autobiography at an early age when her mother is still alive to read and, in some sense, monitor her output. Though Lynn Z. Bloom comments that not only does the "daughter-as-autobiographer become her own mother, she also becomes the re-creator of her maternal parent and the controlling adult in their literary relationship" (292), I think she may minimize the influence of a still-living mother.

Angelou's autobiography, though set largely in the impoverished area of Stamps, Arkansas, during the depression, is pervaded by the same hunger that characterizes the far different circumstances of Sarraute's autobiography. Like Sarraute, Angelou intensely desires her mother's presence, obsessively describes her mother's beautiful body, and continually recognizes that her mother flits just beyond her grasp. Angelou describes her mother in terms that emphasize her evanescence: e.g., as a "pretty kite that floated just above" her head, "a hurricane in its perfect power," "the climbing, falling down colors of a rainbow," a "blithe chick [that] . . . peeps and chirps" or as someone so elusive Maya cannot even put "a finger on her realness" (54, 49, 171, 57). Yet, for all the physical descriptions of her mother in her autobiography, Angelou's emotional/psychological portrayal of her mother remains curiously circumspect.

Comparably, the care with which Dillard screens her autobiographical observations becomes particularly evident as she grows into adolescence. In Dillard's autobiography, her recognition of the hypocrisy and smug affluence of her culture never really comes to a head. Instead, Dillard's wry descriptions of her teenage rebellions lack depth and seem, finally, more like a caricature or burlesque of adolescence. Similarly, Dillard never criticizes her mother's lifestyle and states, unconvincingly: "When I was growing up I didn't really take to Pittsburgh society, and I was happy to throw myself to any other world I could find. But I guess I can't say so, because my family may think that I confuse them with conventional Pittsburgh society people in the 1950s" (70). Why, one wonders, having read the autobiography, *wouldn't* Dillard confuse her family with conventional Pittsburgh society?

In a similar fashion, Angelou also remains silent. In Angelou's case, however, the silence startles. When she and her brother, Bailey, at the ages of three and four, respectively, are "shipped" home to live with their paternal grandmother, Angelou at first describes the incident dispassionately (8). Only several chapters later, when their parents unexpectedly send Christmas presents (after years of not writing or sending gifts), does Angelou reveal her bitterness. Angelou, previously, had protected herself by "picturing" her mother dead: " . . . lying in her coffin . . . . The face was brown, like a big O, and since I couldn't fill in the features I printed M O T H E R across the O, and tears would fall down my cheeks like warm milk" (43). But the arrival of the Christmas presents disrupts Angelou's fantasy and she writes, poignantly:

> The gifts opened the door to questions that neither of us [Angelou and Bailey] wanted to ask. Why did they send us away? and What did we do so wrong? So Wrong? Why, at three and four, did we have tags

put on our arms to be sent by train alone from Long Beach, California, to Stamps, Arkansas, with only the porter to look after us? (Besides, he got off in Arizona). (43)

Yet, a year later, when Angelou finally sees her mother for the first
time since she was sent away, her bitterness immediately drops away.
She is "struck dumb" by her mother's beauty and comments: "I knew instantly why she had sent me away. She was too beautiful to have children" (49, 50). Angelou's prompt adoration of her mother, after the
years of abandonment, becomes, as Selwyn Cudjoe articulates, "increasingly puzzling and unsettling;" consistently Angelou displays "a
daughterly love that the mother does not deserve and that is singularly
unconvincing" (196).

Though—arguably—Angelou merely demonstrates the resiliency of
childhood, a child's desire to love her/his parents despite their actions,
her silence after being raped by her mother's lover, Mr. Freeman, warrants comment. When Angelou is raped (at the age of eight), she feels
her subsequent testimony literally kills Freeman (he is murdered soon
after the trial by Maya's uncles) and she stops speaking altogether. But
Angelou's silence also pervades her later autobiographical reconstruction
of the event. When her mother sends her back home to Momma (Angelou's paternal grandmother), Angelou defends the action: "There is
nothing more appalling than a constantly morose child" and states, unconvincingly, that she "cared less about the trip than about the fact that
Bailey was unhappy, and had no more thought of our destination than if I
had simply been heading for the toilet" (74). Cudjoe similarly comments
on Angelou's reluctance to ever come "to terms with the matriarchal
farce that her biological mother embodies" and also passes his own
judgment on Maya's mother's actions following the rape: e.g., " . . . in
the most shocking callousness one could adopt toward a child, the
mother returns her daughter to Momma because Maya is depressed after
the rape" (198).

Significantly, the only time Angelou does not feel any ambivalence toward her mother is when, as a young child, she is able to imagine her mother dead. Autobiographically speaking, the only *good* mother is a dead mother. To put this less crassly, only a mother already dead does not create a textual problem. Mary McCarthy, though acidly portraying the bulk of her adult relatives in *Memories of a Catholic Girlhood*, writes glowingly of her mother, who died during the influenza epidemic when McCarthy was six. Carolyn Heilbrun—in similar terms—notes while surveying the book *Between Women*, a collection of largely autobiographical essays, that "when a woman sought a female model for self-realization [such as in her mother], she had to find it in a woman who had died . . . ." (65).

Zora Neale Hurston, in her autobiography, *Dust Tracks on a Road*, is consequently able to portray her mother without the tension evident in Dillard and Angelou's autobiographies. After her mother dies when Hurston is nine, Hurston is free to eulogize her mother without implying her mother operated as a role model on anything but a metaphorical level. Speculatively, it would be hard to believe that Hurston would have referred to her mother—domestic and uneducated—as her mentor if she had lived. In fact, Hurston saw herself more in her father, a point she clarifies when she identifies her love of "wandering" as an inheritance from her father (32). Hurston's text, as Nellie McKay observes, is a "'statue' of the 'self' she wishes the world to see" (180). And what Hurston wishes the world to see is her success; her female "models" include culturally dominant women such as Fanny Hurst or Ethel Waters rather than her mother.

Audre Lorde, in her memoir, *Zami: A New Spelling of my Name*, deliberately works against the typical trajectory of autobiography. Lorde refers to her autobiographical project as a "biomythography," a "renaming of her text and her self [that] creates a representational space where homes, identities, and names have mythic qualities" (Gilmore 27). In particular, Lorde mythologizes her mother. Unlike Dillard, Lorde does not depict a childhood of privilege but describes instead her mother's courageous approach to raising a poor, black family in the prejudiced environment of Harlem in the 1930s. In a gesture similar to that of Dillard's, however, Lorde also perceives her mother as *different* and though Lorde acknowledges that while her mother's difference sometimes brings her "pain" it also provides her "a sense of pleasure and specialness that was a positive aspect of feeling set apart" (185). More than once Lorde writes, emphatically, "my mother was different from other women" (185) or "I always knew my mother was different from the other women I knew, Black or white" (183). Like Dillard's mother, Lorde's mother spawns a love of language, of the beauty and sensuality of words, that influences Lorde's career as a writer. More specifically, however, the complex difference Lorde's mother possesses stems from her "power." Her mother power is so obvious other people immediately recognize it as well. Lorde describes how her father "shared decisions and the making of all policy" (185) with her mother—a parity unusual for that time—and how other people automatically deferred to her as well:

> Her public air of in-charge competence was quiet and effective. On the street people deferred to my mother over questions of taste, economy, opinion, quality, not to mention who had the right to the first available seat on the bus . . . . I became aware, early on, that sometimes people would change their actions because of some opinion my mother never uttered, or even particularly cared about. (186)

It is only after Lorde becomes older that she realizes her mother did experience moments of powerlessness. Nevertheless, Lorde's admiration for her mother clearly hinges on her *difference* and again invokes the question raised in discussing Dillard's depiction of her mother: If a mother operates as a role model largely because of her "difference" from other mothers what does this suggest about the value or worth of motherhood in general? While Lorde's mother does seem extraordinary would she remain the focus of Lorde's biomythography if she were not?

Although mothers are portrayed complexly in well-known autobiographies by women of color such as Maya Angelou, Zora Neale Hurston, or Audre Lorde, the mother-daughter relationships between women of color are consistently theorized and generalized as "positive" and autobiographies by women of color are critiqued to conform to this pattern. In autobiography, however, whether mother-daughter relations in women of color are essentially positive or not is not really at issue. Instead, what must be considered is how these relations get represented at the level of text. We may see in Sarraute's obsessive portrayal of her mother's body, in Dillard's strained portrait of her mother, or in Angelou's determined silence about her mother's actions, that what may have been the "real" mother-daughter relationship is not necessarily the subject of autobiography.

As a case in point, the restraint Angelou demonstrates when writing about her mother in *I Know Why the Caged Bird Sings*, contrasts dramatically with the anger she admits in seventeen years later in a 1987 interview/conversation with her long-standing friend, Rosa Guy. Here Angelou demonstrates none of the reticence so puzzling in her autobiography and states emphatically:

> I was very angry. I haven't stopped being angry at a number of things. I saw my mother once between the time I was three and thirteen. As far as I know, I got one letter, one package from her in those tens years with a little white doll. The very idea! I was young and all that but I knew that this was an insult and I convinced myself that she was dead . . . . (5)

Further, Angelou admits that in order to cope with her mother's coldness she made her into a *character*, a construction rather than the real mother "she wanted and needed" (6). Angelou explains how at first "60 per cent of the time I saw her as a character. Then it grew to be 70 per cent. Then 80. And then my own resistance allowed me to accept her as the character" (6). While Angelou's deliberate fictionalization of her mother represents an extreme example, the mother's autobiographical "reality"—whatever that might be—once embodied in text, is always somewhat of a constructed character. Autobiographically, a mother may become whatever her daughter wishes her to be.

Even when the mother plays a central role in a daughter's autobiography, she is *seen* less as a subject than object and portrayed in largely visual terms. To illustrate how emphatically mothers are depicted as beautiful bodies, one need only consider the inverse proposition. How many male autobiographers obsessively describe the bodies of their fathers? To relegate motherhood to the site of spectacle is as efficiently a form of erasure as the erasure of the mother Beauvoir effects with her paternal/maternal, mind/body split.

The position of "mother" in women's autobiographies might be explained by an analogy. In an article about black women, Barbara Johnson explains how, in a tetrapolar graph she has constructed plotting race (white/black) and gender (male/female), the black woman "is both invisible and ubiquitous: never seen in her own right but forever appropriated by the others for their own ends" (168). The black woman becomes, as Michele Wallace argues, placed in the "unspeakable posture of the 'other' of the 'other'" (60). In autobiography—if not in "real" life—a mother is similarly "twice-othered" by autobiographical discourse. She does not speak—her daughter speaks for her—and her representation is further diluted by the constraints of genre, culture, and audience.

If the daughter's depiction of her mother gives us only a partial slant, what is the view from the other side? That is, what do mothers as autobiographers have to say about motherhood? And, further, how much has even been said? As Susan Rubin Suleiman points out, mothers have not only been systematically erased by both men and women, but have, themselves, historically been silent. Suleiman remarks, summarizing Tillie Olsen, that "mothers who have been 'full-time' writers have been, with very few exceptions, childless during all or most of their writing lives" (358). By examining the flipside of women's autobiography—the lesser discussed autobiographies by mothers—we may, at least, learn enough, as Suleiman posits, to ask "the right questions" about "the inner discourse of a mother" (358).

IV

The Mother Speaks: A Really Bloody Show

Most of what has been, is, between mothers, daughters, and in motherhood, in daughterhood, has never been recorded, nor (even as yet) written with comprehension in our own voices, out of our own lives and truths. What does exist is small, perhaps the smallest portion of all literature . . . . Least present *is* work written by mothers themselves (although each year sees more). Whatever the differences now (including literacy, small families), for too many of the old, old old reasons, few mothers while in the everyday welter of motherhood life, or after, are writing it. That everyday welter, the sense of its troublous context, the voice of the mother herself, are the largest absences in this book. And elsewhere.

—Tillie Olsen, *Mother to Daughter: Daughter to Mother*

The Order of Things and Mothers

In a critical theory seminar he was conducting, Herbert Blau described an article he wrote entitled, "The Bloody Show and the Eye of Prey." The article treated his thoughts through his wife's "bloody show," labor, and the subsequent birth of their daughter. It is, without a doubt, a highly theoretical and sophisticated text, yet I could not help wondering how it would have been received if it had been written from a wife's perspective—even Herbert Blau's wife [Kathleen Woodward], who is also a noted scholar. The same article, written from the mother's viewpoint would have then had, as its implicit subtext: just another woman telling just another labor story. Though Blau begins his article by humorously asserting his position as an *actual* father rather than as a paternal authority in the Lacanian sense, his "significance" and "signification" as a father lend authority nonetheless.

As a case in point, in the same critical theory seminar we discussed "Stabat Mater" by Julia Kristeva. Kristeva's article, written with a "deliberate typographical fragmentation of the page," presents Kristeva's personal experience as a mother juxtaposed next to the more formally written main body of the text (Moi 160). In the left-hand portion of the text, Kristeva writes of her maternal experience in a fluid, semiotic style of writing that may, as some critics posit, be her attempt to show the symbolic order's disruption by the "wild space" of the pre-Oedipal chora. In poetic, flowing language, for example, Kristeva describes the complex connection/disconnection inherent in the mother/child relationship:

> motherhood destines us to a demented *jouissance* that is answered, by chance, by the nursling's laughter in the sunny waters of the ocean. What connection is there between it and myself? No connection, except for that overflowing laughter where one senses the collapse of some ringing, subtle, fluid identity or other, softly buoyed by the waves. (179–80)

No one in the seminar seemed to know what to say about Kristeva's essay. In fact, the seminar's ensuing discussion remained strained and uncomfortable until one woman commented that she found Kristeva's personal writing about her son's birth "sappy." Though it was a "co-ed" seminar, nearly all the women—none of the men commented at this juncture—immediately and vehemently agreed that Kristeva's maternal writing was, indeed, sappy.

Actually, the point was not whether Kristeva's quasi-*écriture féminine* was or was not sappy. More remarkable was the vehemence with which the women in the seminar attacked and rapidly dissociated themselves from the maternal position. Clearly, Kristeva's desire to foreground her position as a mother and a body bound into an intensely loving and erotic relationship with her newborn son made the women in the seminar uneasy. Terming the writing "sappy" shifted the ground of criticism away from the *content* of Kristeva's maternal writing to its style. By focusing instead on the "style," the women effected an erasure since Kristeva's "ideas" would not have to be entertained if we agreed that the marginalized, semiotic writing was inferior in the first place. Of course, by erasing the semiotic writing from consideration the women could also bypass any discussions about motherhood as a *real* versus theoretical experience. Ironically in the non-semiotic portion of the essay Kristeva comments on this very erasure. By not bothering to critique motherhood thoroughly, "feminism circumvents the real experience that fantasy overshadows. The result?—A negation or rejection of motherhood by some avant-garde feminist groups. Or else an acceptance—conscious or not—of its traditional representations by the great mass of people, women and men" (161).

The critical commentary on "Stabat Mater" pretty much parallels the reception it received in the critical theory seminar I described. In both Toril Moi and Dan Latimer's introduction to "Stabat Mater," they accord Kristeva's maternal, semiotic writing one line while devoting the rest of their introductions to the main part—the important part—of Kristeva's text, i.e., where she writes in the traditional academic style of an intellectual daughter.

Though Susan Rubin Suleiman comments, re-affirming the sentiments of many other theorists, that "Mothers don't write, they are written" (357), what might also be considered is whether mothers are heard when they *do* write. And, more importantly, do we *want* or even know how to hear mothers? In my critical theory seminar, it was quite clear that we did not want to hear Kristeva-as-mother but Kristeva-as-daughter. In autobiography, where the self is foregrounded, we have seen how the mother's [textual] representation has been diluted, distorted, and/or erased by their daughters. What happens when the mother tries to represent herself?

Mom's Best Sellers: The Housebroken, Domesticated Gothics of Betty MacDonald, Shirley Jackson, and Erma Bombeck

> I love the house here as though it were an entity, a living and active presence, aloof but benign, its being in a tension of desire with my being, a body other than but like my body. . . . . The passion that I feel for this house will mold my relationship to every other space I occupy . . . . As with all desirable entities, I fear the house as well as love it.
>
> —Nancy Mairs, *Remembering the Bone House*

If the daughter as autobiographer finds identification with the mother risky, the risks increase exponentially when the daughter attempts to speak from the position of mother. A model literally does not exist. Or rather, the mothers that get published and read by large audiences have famous fathers, famous husbands, famous children, or are autobiographies that aim to be morally instructive or that center on a single dramatic incident. In other words, the position of mother in all these autobiographies is subordinate to the content of the autobiography itself.

The best-selling autobiographies of mothers concentrating on motherhood itself comprise a sub-genre of their own. These "motherhood" autobiographies share a remarkably similar ironic stance: e.g., Shirley Jackson's *Life Among the Savages* and *Raising Demons*, Jean Kerr's *Please Don't Eat the Daisies*, Betty MacDonald's *Onions in the Stew* and *The Egg and I*, Mary Kuczkir's *My Dishtowel Flies at Half-Mast*, Teresa Bloomingdale's *Sense and Momsense*, and any of various books by Erma Bombeck: *Family: The Ties That Bind and Gag, Motherhood: The Second Oldest Profession, Just Wait Till You Have Children of Your Own*, or *The Grass Is Always Greener Over the Septic Tank*.

But irony is a defense mechanism, the protection of self. In the case of what could be termed "funny mother" autobiographies, the woman deflects any attacks on the position of motherhood by rendering that position slightly ridiculous in advance. The tone is genial and amused while the wittily self-deprecating style neatly underscores the mother's [real] intelligence. Accordingly, Shirley Jackson begins her autobiography, *Life Among the Savages*, with a calculated description of books and brood: "Our house is old, and noisy and full. When we moved into it we had two children and about five thousand books; I expect that when we finally overflow and move out again we will have perhaps twenty children and easily half a million books . . . ." (1).

By strategically packaging their autobiographies into a series of wry misadventures and foibles, writers like Bombeck and Jackson ensure an audience but actually distance themselves from themselves, from their position as mothers. Oddly, most of the humorous/domestic autobiographies begin similarly. Betty MacDonald's *The Egg and I* and *Onions in the Stew*, Erma Bombeck's *The Grass Is Always Greener Over the Septic Tank*, Shirley Jackson's *Raising Demons* and *Life Among the Savages* and Jean Kerr's *Please Don't Eat the Daisies* (particularly in its screen adaptation) all share the same premise: a family moves into a new (and generally very old and dilapidated) house.

Conceivably, moving into a new house could provide the means of inserting "adventure" into what might otherwise be a humdrum plot. The house, usually a monstrosity, offers a challenge to the mother who must somehow tame the house and make it livable. But the autobiographer/mother may have other reasons for using this particular plot pattern.

In *Civilization and Its Discontents*, Freud argues that a home operates as an alternative mother: ". . . the dwelling-place was a substitute for the mother's womb" (38). Similarly, Claire Kuhane, in "The Gothic Mirror," posits that the home or "castle" of Gothic fiction operates as a mother substitute but here, rather than offering the safety of the womb, suggests the power of the phallic mother's body: "[a] body, awesome and powerful, which is both our habitat and our prison . . . [a body] imagina-

tively linked to the realm of Nature, figuring the forces of life and death"
(337).

For a woman, the association with the maternal house is more complex since she does not effect as clear a break with the mother as a man
does during the course of maturation. Accordingly, Kuhane asserts that
"the heroine's active exploration of the Gothic house in which she is
trapped is also an exploration of her relation to the maternal body that
she shares, with all its connotations of power over and vulnerability to
forces from within and without" (338).

In classic Gothic fiction, the house is generally a castle, labyrinthine
in design and sinister in aspect. The heroine, often a young woman
whose mother has died, wanders helplessly in the house's secret pas-
sageways and hidden rooms (Kuhane 334). The house of domestic autobiographies proves similarly daunting. Here, however, the macabre tone
of Gothic fiction gives way to hyperbole and humor.

In having the house occupy the space of the mother, an autobiogra-
pher/mother de-phallicizes her own position. The mother, in fact, becomes a "daughter." The autobiographer/mother, by pitting herself—
humorously but unsuccessfully—against the challenges the maternal
house presents, is able to revert back to the daughter's role. What the
daughter/autobiographer/mother in her "domesticated" Gothic cannot escape, however, is the undercurrent Kuhane suggests. However much the
daughter/mother may desire to dissociate herself from the maternal
house, it is always an exploration of her own body and her own fears as
well.

Nevertheless, the ploy of Bombeck *et al.* represents a canny maneuver. If the all-powerful, phallic mother is feared and hated, the mother of
the domesticated Gothic—defeated by house, children, and husband—is
downright lovable. In *The Grass Is Always Greener Over the Septic
Tank*, Erma Bombeck helplessly tells her husband:

> . . . every time I push down the toaster, the garage door goes up. The
> hot-water heater is hooked up to the garden hose and I am sautéing

the lawn. The sliding-glass doors don't slide. The wall heats up when I turn on the porch light. The hall toilet does not accept tissue . . . . I have a sign on our front door reading, 'OUT OF ORDER! PLEASE USE HOUSE NEXT DOOR!' (50).

Betty MacDonald, in *The Egg and I*, describes her new home in similarly despairing terms. When she and her husband first see the home, MacDonald comments how it looks "distressingly forlorn . . . the buildings grayed with weather . . . the fences collapsing, the windows gaping" (44). Satirically, MacDonald states it was the type of house that prompts people to comment, "'Look at the picturesque old place!' then quickly drive by toward something not quite so picturesque, but warmer and nearer to civilization" (44).

Though Bombeck and Kerr manage to keep a nearly perfect balance between humor and hysteria, Jackson and MacDonald's narrative voice betrays more desperation. Typically, Bombeck never falters; she unerringly maintains her highly marketable stance of good-natured defeat. Her distance from any sort of domestic competence is underscored when she describes the difference between the Super Mom and herself (an Interim Mother). The Super Moms " . . . were faster than a speeding bullet, more powerful than a harsh laxative, and able to leap six shopping carts on double stamp day. She was a drag for all seasons" ("Septic Tank" 200). In contrast, Bombeck and the Interim Mothers " . . . were just biding their time until the children were grown. They never gave their right name at PTA meetings, hid candy under the dish towel so the kids would never find it, had newspapers lining the cupboard shelves that read, 'MALARIA STOPS WORK ON THE CANAL'" ("Septic Tank" 201).

Unforgivably, the Super Mom masters the maternal house. Bombeck, for example, describes the house of a Super Mom she calls Estelle. Although Estelle has just moved into her new house, Bombeck notes, incredulously, that, "The furniture was shining and in place, the mirrors and pictures were hung, there was not a cardboard box in sight, the books

were on the shelves, [and] there were fresh flowers on the kitchen table"
("Septic Tank" 201). Bombeck's humorous advice to Estelle—to be less
"perfect" so that she could be one of them—has an edge to it nevertheless. The Super Mom isn't really liked.

MacDonald ostensibly presents herself as an Interim Mother, but
her desire to display her Super Mom competence repeatedly unsettles her
narrative stance. MacDonald reveals the artificiality of making the Super
Mom an either/or position. In reality, Super Moms and Interim Mothers
operate on a sliding scale; one woman's Super Mom is another woman's
disaster. Though female relationships are often described in sisterly
terms, women's relationships may also replicate a mother-daughter dynamic, with the woman currently perceived as being more competent occupying the mother's position. Domestic autobiographies, however, attempt to keep the fluctuating Super Mom/Interim Mother relationship
static; the Super Moms are cast as the autobiography's villains while the
autobiographer remains in the popular, daughterly position of an Interim
Mother.

Like Bombeck, MacDonald also denounces the Super Mom, who
materializes as a woman named Birdie Hicks in *The Egg and I*. Birdie
Hicks' house is perfect and creates an impossible standard for Mac-
Donald, who comments that "Working within the sacred bounds of Mrs.
Hicks' cleanliness proved such a strong impetus for a while that I found
myself going after corners in my own house with pins and washing the
face of the kitchen clock" (141). However, MacDonald does take pains
to establish relative mastery. In contrast to the ramshackle house of their
neighbors, Ma and Pa Kettle, MacDonald's house shines.

Though MacDonald articulates her anger about some of her other
neighbors, the kitchen stove, the weather, the lack of plumbing, and other
less important problems, MacDonald's book—ostensibly humorous—
seethes with unspoken resentments. Significantly, MacDonald begins
her book in the daughter's position, by summarizing the advice her
mother has handed down to her: "Along with teaching us that lamb must
be cooked with garlic and that a lady never scratches her head or spits,

my mother taught my sisters and me that it is a wife's bounded duty to see that her husband is happy in his work" (11).

Despite her ironic tone, MacDonald refers to her mother's advice several times. It is also clear that her mother's opinions on wifely duty influence MacDonald to travel with her new husband, Bob, to the desolate chicken farm she describes in *The Egg and I*. Her mother's party line: i.e., make your husband happy and do what he wants—prompts MacDonald to acquiesce to her husband's seemingly endless list of demands and chores. If MacDonald resents her mother's advice, she does not say so.

MacDonald's resentment towards her husband is less covert. Although she never refuses the life Bob maps out for her, in many of her descriptions of their work on the farm she sounds like a woman on the verge of desperation or even madness. The farm's rampant productivity threatens to engulf MacDonald. Her work—already staggering—increases when their baby chicks arrive, at a time when MacDonald herself is pregnant. MacDonald describes the endless, cyclical process of rising early ("Up at four"), and rushing from one domestic duty inside her house to rushing outside to feed the baby chicks. Exhausted, MacDonald describes how her hellish schedule continues "on and on through the day," a life she sums up by stating: "I felt as if I were living in a nightmare, fleeing down the track on front of an onrushing locomotive" (106).

The farm's obscene fertility accelerates MacDonald's workload and becomes a metaphor for her despair. When she returns from the hospital with her new baby, the farm has been cranking out more and more life in her absence:

> When I came home from the hospital after two weeks of blissful rest, everything on the ranch had been busily producing and I was greeted by the squealing of baby pigs, the squeaking of baby goslings, the baaing of a heifer calf, the mewing of tiny kittens, the yelping of a puppy and the stronger yelping of the chicks. All the small eat-often

screamers were assigned to my care and I found that feeding them
and Bob and me was a perpetual task. (106)

Despite the book's many humorous anecdotes, MacDonald's often
vivid descriptions of her exhaustion coupled with her inability to communicate her unhappiness to her stolid husband, Bob, provide an undercurrent of horror. By the end of the book, in MacDonald's most overt
statement of discontent, she describes how she had omitted telling her
husband about a strange woman who terrified her earlier that day: "I
didn't even try to convey my terror because I knew by then that Bob and
I were poles apart as far as emotions were concerned" (274). Though
Bob appears difficult at best, repeatedly MacDonald cites her own short-
comings. Instead of focusing on the astonishing amount of work she
does accomplish, MacDonald looks instead at all the work that does not
get done because of her "usual bad management" (188). And this is supposed to be funny.

Why do women—and particularly mothers—disparage and often
ridicule their own work? Jean Kerr, for example, in her autobiographical
book, *How I Got to Be Perfect*, ironically describes her inability to pack
her children's cold lunches:

> Another woman could make a tasty sandwich spread by mixing
> evaporated milk and mayonnaise with some curry powder. But I lack
> the dash for this kind of experimentation. For that matter I lack the
> curry powder, and—what is more to the point—I lack qualities of
> leadership. Yes, I do. I'm an unfit mother and a rotten housekeeper,
> as shiftless and improvident as a character out of *God's Little Acres*.
> (102)

Though Kerr's anecdote deals with a trivial matter and *is* funny,
mothers almost automatically represent themselves in apologetic terms. I
did. When my third son was born, my oldest boy was less than two-and-
one-half years of age and my second son was thirteen months old. All
three boys were still in diapers and all three were on different schedules.

My third boy was born with a complete cleft of the lip and hard and soft palate, a condition requiring several surgeries. I nursed him indirectly, first pumping out the milk and then feeding him with a bottle equipped with a special nipple that had to be aimed down his throat or he would choke. Feeding him took hours every day and hours every night. Often, during the year after he was born, my hands would shake, involuntarily. Nevertheless, when people came to visit, I would joke about my moderately messy house, and throw out one-liners about my lack of domesticity. But I wasn't inept; I was exhausted.

Nancy A. Walker's excellent study, *A Very Serious Thing: Women's Humor and American Culture*, goes a long way toward explaining how women use humor to write their lives. Walker argues that the self-deprecatory stance of writers of domestic humor is actually subversive:

> The humorous text, which appears to surrender to the status quo, carries within it the codes that members of the group recognize as part of their common heritage. While superficially accepting the assessment of the dominant culture—e.g., women are frivolous, gossipy, inept—on a deeper level women's humor calls into question the values that have led to those assessments. (36)

Compared to what would have been acceptable in the nineteenth or early twentieth centuries, Bombeck's satiric comments on motherhood and housework do indicate progress. On the other hand, it is arguable whether Bombeck's writing is really subversive or merely reinforces the status quo. Bombeck might ridicule carpools, suburbia, and the PTA, but year after year she wrote her earlier best sellers from the same position. There is no sense in the writing for which Bombeck is best known that she plans to escape the trials and tribulations of suburban Mom-dom.

Nevertheless, Bombeck's situation warrants further comment. Just as Kristeva's attempt to write from the position of a mother (rather than an intellectual daughter) in "Stabat Mater" was not well received critically, Bombeck faced a similar challenge when she attempted to switch "roles." Bombeck was adored as a domestic humorist and self-deprecating mother, but she had a much harder time being taken seriously when she expressed increasingly feminist views later in her career. As Susan Edwards explains in her biography of Bombeck entitled *Erma Bombeck: A Life in Humor* (1997), despite the fact that Bombeck worked very hard in supporting the Equal Rights Amendment, Bombeck often felt the movement was elitist and catered to a certain type of woman, i.e., intellectual non-mothers. Accordingly, Bombeck comments—with appropriate irony—that her contributions were never really solicited by the women's liberation movement:

> They picked out the American housewife as the battleground for the whole movement, but they didn't invite us to the war. I would personally like to wring the neck of whoever invented that phrase 'just a housewife' because, basically, that's what I still am . . . . No one ever asked me to make a stand. Which I think is fairly typical. We housewives were the last to be asked what we wanted. That's probably why the amendment is in trouble today. Finally the feminists are coming to us and saying, "We can't do it without you." (qtd. in Edwards 128).

Bombeck raises an interesting point. Just as Kristeva—accepted as an intellectual—could theorize about motherhood but was rejected when she tried to occupy the mother's position, Bombeck—labeled as "just a housewife"—was often rejected when she wrote or spoke intellectually about the very position she occupied. In short, Bombeck charges that many feminists never listened to the very women (those perceived as unliberated housewives) they proposed to free. To illustrate this point by an analogy, in *Williams Obstetrics*, still considered the "bible" of obstetrical medicine, the authors (all male) continue to suggest that the pain women experience in childbirth is often more psychological than physical. The text also suggests that the ideal patient, i.e., one who trusts her doctor completely, will deliver her baby painlessly and easily. Accordingly, all five of the last editions begin their discussion on pain with this question: "Is labor easy because a woman is calm, or is she calm because her labor is easy?" (19th ed. 371). The question itself raises a couple of implications: that easy labors are somewhat common and that labor pain is dependent on the woman's emotional status. Since most women do experience pain in childbirth and the reasons why labor is painful seem obvious, the implication that the pain might be psychogenic is startling. Oddly, editions before 1950 did not debate the reality of labor pain. The fifth edition of *Williams Obstetrics*—published in 1923—clearly outlines the physical cause for pain in labor and refers to the pain as "very severe" or even "almost insupportable" (254). Further, the fifth edition contradicts the suggestion that easy labors are common and states, in fact, that only in rare instances will labor will "entirely painless" (254). While the standpoint on pain in the later versus the earlier editions of *Williams* may seem insignificant, the shift in ideology serves to make women feel that labor pain is abnormal. Amazingly, rather than interviewing *women* who have experienced or were experiencing labor, the authors used a study by a (male) British obstetrician, Grantly Dick-Read. Read, who conducted his study in 1944, could have interviewed women during and following labor, but instead merely *observes* them. *Williams* quotes the portion of Read's study where "after scrutinizing many cases," he concluded that "Fear is in some way the chief pain-producing agent in otherwise normal labor" (17th ed. 405).

It is evident that the authors felt the second-hand observations of a male physician were more reliable than what they could learn from women themselves. Apparently, women could not objectively assess their pain or their emotional state. Similarly, Bombeck and other "housewives" could not objectively assess the degree to which they felt oppressed; they needed academic feminists to "translate" and "theorize" their position.

Interestingly, Bombeck, though loved as a harmless writer of "funny mother" stories, found her fairly conservative feminist views under attack by mainstream culture as well. As Susan Edwards notes in her biography of Bombeck, the "lieutenant governor of a southern state said she [Bombeck] should be at home having babies" while a "Salt Lake City bookstore removed her books from their shelves" (134). Clearly, Bombeck's emerging feminism elicited some discomfort from both her former fans as well as many feminists.

However, Bombeck's best liked writing does not provide many solutions. Although Nancy Walker theorizes that women's humor presents a subversive argument, Bombeck's thesis often remains submerged. Judged in terms of it succeeding as a subversive message to other mothers, Bombeck's most popular writing often falls short. What action, if any, does Bombeck propose mothers take? In practice, Bombeck does not seem to advocate rebellion so much as resignation. A mother's job, she says, is impossible, unmanageable, and basically laughable; only a dimwit (i.e., a Super Mom) would take it too seriously. And, perhaps, this *is* Bombeck's message, a message that could be summed up by replacing the word "marriage" with the word *motherhood* in a comment Bombeck made when she was asked what she would do if she had her life to live over again:

> "I would be more relaxed. [Motherhood] is basically out of your control. You're a boat in a storm. You just ride it out and hope the boat holds together. I used to think I could change things like birth, death, and struggle. You can't. You rise above them." (qtd. in Edwards, 208–9)

While Bombeck's message of acceptance provides comfort for women whose lives are *acceptable*, it does not address the lives of mothers whose lives are not, e.g., women who are poor, abused, single, overwhelmed, overworked, and so forth. And, for mothers who feel they cannot accomplish motherhood even at its most minimal level, the image of the Super Mom, our modern "Angel in the House," provides a particularly grim reminder of their inadequacy. Walker also cites the prevalence of the Super Mom in women's domestic humor but concludes that the image of "impossibly capable women in women's humor suggests that rather than endorsing or even accepting these extremes of women's behavior, the authors are rejecting the cultural forces that have created them" (65). While the authors themselves may be rejecting and critiquing the social catalysts that created the Super Mom, how many mothers can ignore the guilt the Super Mom inspires?

But who, precisely, is the Super Mom? Ellen Goodman, in an autobiographical essay entitled, "Your Better Basic Supermother" offers this introduction to the subject:

> The Supermother, for those of you who haven't met her, is that Perfect Person against whom we compare ourselves in order to fully experience failure, not to mention self-loathing, and a complex labeled inferiority. She is the lady we carry around in our heads just for the guilt of it. (180)

The Super Mom, that "perfect," powerful person "we carry around in our heads" may be none other than our own mother or a surrogate—as omnipotent as she was in our earliest memories—and who serves as the sub-ur-pre-text of all motherhood.

Somewhat perversely, then, the Super Mom may also have a positive function. The Super Mom's competence—her imagined phallic power—allows the mother/autobiographer to remain in the daughter's position. When I had my first child—whom I now recognize was a "very easy baby"—my husband, noting my success with our son, suddenly treated me like an oracle of maternal wisdom. His deference was both flattering and frightening. I did not have *all* the answers and felt uncomfortable being treated as though I did. My neighbor, a Super Mom by virtue of having five sons to my one, soon intervened to let me know all the things I was doing wrong. Surprisingly, I took my neighbor's advice with relief as well as resentment. Her critical commentary—e.g., Don't you think the baby's dressed too warmly? Shouldn't he be on cereal by now? You're going to use *disposable* diapers?—gave me the opportunity to move back into the daughter's position like a pair of comfortable shoes. I could take her advice or resent it, depending on whether I wanted to be like a dutiful or a rebellious daughter. Either way, however, I got a reprieve from being a mother.

Beneath the humor of domestic autobiographies like those of Mac-Donald, and Jackson, is their resentment at being irrevocably thrust into the mother's position, no longer able to be mothered themselves. Conversely, Jane Lazarre, in *The Mother Knot*, foregrounds her anger and describes her resentment as she watches her husband and her mother-in-law pay more attention to her new son, Benjamin, than they do to her:

> When James came home from school, he hovered over the baby, trying to help his mother, or he walked Benjamin himself as Marie prepared dinner. I held back my tears, choked on the words of need trying to push themselves out of my mouth. I hated Marie and James for worrying so much about the goddamn baby when I wanted to be held, stroked, rocked. (33)

But the writers of humorous, domestic autobiographies do not express this resentment, nor do they express the gripping fear many mothers experience when they realize that their job—in its barest terms—is to keep their child alive.

In her autobiographical work, *Life Among the Savages*, Shirley Jackson carefully skirts around the topic of death. Though she matter-of-factly describes her son's near-fatal accident, her shock and disorientation nevertheless emerge clearly:

> Two days before his eighth birthday, Laurie rode his bike around a bend, directly into the path of a car. I can remember with extraordinary clarity that one of the people in the crowd which gathered handed me a lighted cigarette, I can remember saying reasonably that we all ought not to be standing in the middle of the road . . . . (162)

But Jackson edits out her terror. Although she does not learn until late in the night following the accident that her son would be all right, Jackson keeps her tone light and controlled. Jackson ends the incident wryly by describing how Laurie was able to gain people's rapt attention with spellbinding renditions of the accident.

In the Gothic fiction for which Jackson is better known, she is able to construct chilling tales from events as prosaic as a chicken-eating dog ("The Renegade") or a visit to the dentist ("The Tooth"). Conversely, her son's accident—potentially far more terrifying—is transformed into a funny story. The humor of domestic autobiography rests on the author's ability to provide a one-sided picture of motherhood. Accordingly, the heroine of domestic autobiography explores the maternal house very carefully; if she encounters death or despair, she must not write it. Popular mothers are hilarious, not hysterical. Nevertheless, domestic humor overlays domestic horror like thin gauze. Charlotte Perkins Gilman and Maxine Hong Kingston demonstrate how closely allied motherhood and madness can be.

Strategies of Transcendence:
Charlotte Perkins Gilman and Maxine Hong Kingston

> I believe that utopias are not embodiments of universal human values, but are reactive; that is, they supply in fiction what their authors believe society . . . and/or women, lack in the here-and-now. The positive values stressed in the stories can reveal to us what, in the authors' eyes, is wrong with our own society. Thus if the stories are family/communal in feeling, we may pretty safely guess that the authors see our society as isolating people from one another, especially (to judge from the number of all-female utopias in the group) women to women.
>
> —Joanna Russ, "Recent Feminist Utopias"

In Claire Kuhane's article, "The Gothic Mirror," cited earlier in the chapter, she explains how the house in Shirley Jackson's Gothic work, *The Haunting of Hill House*, is "an image of the mother" and that the "nursery is designated the most haunted room" (341). Significantly,

Charlotte Perkins Gilman chooses the nursery of a "colonial mansion" (which the protagonist also calls a "haunted house") as the setting for her famous short story, "The Yellow Wallpaper" (9).

"The Yellow Wallpaper" depicts a young woman's intense postpartum depression and eventual descent into madness. The story parallels, in many ways, the events Gilman narrates in her autobiography, *The Living of Charlotte Perkins Gilman*. In her autobiography, Gilman first presents her physically and mentally vigorous childhood and adolescence. In marked contrast, marriage, pregnancy, childbirth, and motherhood depress Gilman and completely deplete her energies. Her postpartum depression, then diagnosed as "nervous prostration," Gilman describes as a "constant dragging weariness miles below zero. Absolute incapacity. Absolute misery. To the spirit it was as if one were an armless, legless, eyeless voiceless cripple" (91).

In the autobiography, Gilman's husband is an artist, her house is modest, and the child she bears is a girl. Her short story, "The Yellow Wallpaper," published in 1892, predates her autobiography (1935) by forty-three years. Though written just a few years after the birth of Gilman's daughter, her short story contains significant differences from her autobiographical account. In "The Yellow Wallpaper," the house—the maternal body—is massive and slightly decaying. The protagonist not only is subordinate to the maternal house but actually infantilized by being confined in the nursery, a large, garishly papered room with bars on the windows. The protagonist's husband, though well-intentioned, is more arrogant than Gilman depicts her own husband, Charles Walter Stetson, and is a doctor rather than an artist. The protagonist's infant child is a boy. Though Gilman, in her autobiography, states she got "as far as one could go and still get back" from becoming insane (121), the protagonist in her short story goes completely mad.

In short, Gilman took the details from her own life, already dismal enough, and magnified them to create a chilling story in the Gothic vein. By making the protagonist's husband a doctor, Gilman links him to technology, logos, and the rational world of Dr. S. Weir Mitchell, the famous

Philadelphia neurologist whose "rest cure" nearly kills Gilman and drives her fictional prototype mad. Changing the baby's gender to a boy aligns him more closely to the father as well as emphasizing the theme of male dominance Gilman is trying to project. The fictional house's promotion to a "colonial mansion" of "ancestral halls" (9) from the more prosaic home Gilman describes in her autobiography accentuates the story's Gothic structure.

If dissociating from the maternal house in a pose of wry incompetence marks the Interim Mother while mastering the maternal house typifies the Super Mom, Gilman's protagonist demonstrates another route of action. Gilman's protagonist is cut off from any active domestic participation with the house (in compliance with the "rest cure") and confined to the home's former nursery. The woman in Gilman's story understands—on some level—that her confinement in the house is designed to create a docile body: "[In the Gothic genre] the heroine is compelled to resume a quiescent, socially acceptable role or to be destroyed" (Kuhane 342). The story's narrator—haunted by the women she sees (or imagines) trapped in the room's yellow wallpaper—shreds the wallpaper from the room and by the story's end has become completely insane. In brief, given the options of conformity or rebellion, Gilman's protagonist chooses destruction.

A heroine's complete assimilation into the maternal house may lead to madness, death, and/or suicide by breaking down the boundaries of subjectivity between self and other, daughter and mother. But the Gothic structure's maternal center is also a source of power, and as critics have variously interpreted Gilman's story, the protagonist has been viewed as victorious in her escape from the ordered patriarchal world in which she was expected to conform. Yet this victory remains dubious. In our world—patriarchal or otherwise—the reliance on symbol is so ingrained that its rejection renders one without signification, outside interpretation, and completely "othered." Or dead, as Jane Gallop explains, discussing the theories of Julia Kristeva and Luce Irigaray:

> What if Irigaray were to let go of the rigid, fragile, arbitrary distinction between me and you, daughter and mother? According to Julia Kristeva, woman needs language, the paternal, symbolic order, to protect herself from the lack of distinction from the mother. As long as Irigaray speaks, given the rules of grammar, a first and second person can be distinguished. The breakdown of these differences is mortally threatening. (115)

Gilman's protagonist enacts the mortally threatening double bind of eluding symbolic discourse. Her complete retreat into the maternal house, into a pre-symbolic state of non-differentiation we can only read as madness, removes her from the active world. And yet, impossibly and paradoxically, she *writes* her madness. To tell us of her madness—her removal from the world of symbol and logos—the narrator must still use language.

However, Gilman does provide a more positive escape than madness from the cultural restraints imposed on marriage and motherhood. In Gilman's later utopian books: *Moving the Mountain* (1911), *Herland* (1915), and its sequel, *With Her in Ourland* (1916), she fashions a literal "super" mom, a mother endowed with powers that transcend reality. In *Herland*, where Gilman describes her utopian world most completely, the women give birth parthenogenetically, without mating. Their world remains entirely female since the women bear only daughters.

Within the fantastic scope of *Herland*, Gilman is able to solve the problems of motherhood that could not be reconciled in her own life. *All* the women of *Herland* desire maternity—to bear children—but only a few women are considered skilled enough to actually rear the children. Thus, motherhood is divided. Maternity is an innate urge, while the ability to raise children successfully is a learned skill. In *Herland*, Gilman finds a textual resolution to the grinding distress motherhood brought to her narrator in "The Yellow Wallpaper" as well as to Gilman in her own life. As one of the women of *Herland* explains to a male visitor:

almost every woman values her maternity above everything else. Each girl holds it close and dear, an exquisite joy, a crowning honor, the most intimate, most personal, most precious thing. That is, the child-rearing has come to be with us a culture so profoundly studied, practiced with such subtlety and skill, that the more we love our children the less we are willing to trust that process to unskilled hands—even our own. (83)

In *Herland*, then, Gilman offers a special twist on the Super Mother. Super Mothers emerge in the form of the women selected to rear the children as well as in the form of "Over Mothers," the very few women who are allowed to bear more than one child. By elevating childrearing to a learned, specialized skill, Gilman negates the censure (our) society generally accords to an unsuccessful mother. Most mothers, Gilman would appear to be saying, are not equipped to raise their own children; childrearing is not a given, but a gift.

In Gilman's own life, as evidenced in her autobiography, *The Living of Charlotte Perkins Gilman*, the problems of maternity and motherhood are not as readily resolved. Although much of Gilman's previous writing, both fictional and non-fictional, attempts to work out the problems of mothering, Gilman's autobiography records her uneasy relationship to motherhood nonetheless. In the autobiography, the narrative progresses at full tilt until the birth of Gilman's first child. Although Gilman's description of her breakdown and initial attempts to succeed as a mother is vivid and compelling, the rest of the narrative is marked by reticence.

Gilman's decision to relinquish the custody of her daughter, Katharine, to her father creates a textual abyss Gilman cannot overcome. Following Katharine's departure, the rest of Gilman's autobiography becomes lifeless, dwindling into impersonal, disjointed descriptions of various trips and speeches she makes around the country. However successful Gilman's actual life may have been, she is unable to translate her success on a textual level. Gilman herself seemed aware of the discrepancy between her life and her beliefs. Accordingly, Ann J. Lane, in her biography of Gilman, *To Herland and Beyond* (1990), quotes Gilman making the following self-assessment: "I must not forget to apply to my-self the truth I preach to others" (186). Paradoxically, the mothering al-ternatives (e.g., the guilt-free giving of your child to a better caretaker or communal childrearing) Gilman valorized in theory, she did not fully extend to herself in practice.

In the "autofiction," *The Woman Warrior: Memoirs of a Girlhood Among Ghosts*, Maxine Hong Kingston seems similarly caught between alternatives. Despite the fact that Kingston narrates from the daughter's position, the first two stories in her autobiography—stories handed down to her by her own mother—present completely opposite accounts of motherhood. In the first story, "No Name Woman," told to Kingston by her mother as some sort of warning, Kingston learns the story of her aunt, whose name must never be spoken. When Kingston's aunt commits adultery and subsequently bears her lover's baby, the villagers stone the family's house, kill their animals, and destroy their belongings. The next morning, her aunt and the baby are found "plugging up the family well" (5). Kingston's mother ends the story with the moral: "Now that you have started to menstruate, what happened to her could happen to you. Don't humiliate us. You wouldn't want to be forgotten as if you had never been born" (5). Motherhood, the story suggests, carries with it the possibility of shame and erasure.

Conversely, in "White Tigers," Kingston's mother also tells the story of Fa Mu Lan, the Chinese woman warrior of the book's title. In this story, however, Kingston not only identifies with the character—as she did in the story about her aunt—but actually envisions herself as the woman warrior. Here, as in Gilman's utopian book, *Herland*, mother-hood is blissfully achieved [only] within a fantastic context. The woman warrior disguises herself as a man and leads men from one victorious battle to another. Fa Mu Lan is able to transcend usual womanly limita-tions: "Menstrual days did not interrupt my training; I was as strong as on any other day" (36).

Her life is similarly unhindered by pregnancy. Fa Mu Lan conceals the pregnancy under her armor and "rode back to the thickest part of the fighting" immediately after giving birth (47). When her son is a month old, Fa Mu Lan returns the baby to her husband's family and resumes her role as "female avenger" (51). Only after some time has passed—her son is much older—and Fa Mu Lan has avenged her family, does she return, and announce to her husband's family: "Now my public duties are finished . . . . I will stay with you, doing farmwork and housework, and giving you more sons" (54). As Kingston ends the story, dreaming of how they would "make a legend" of her "perfect filiality" (54), she abruptly shifts back to the harsh contrast of her autobiographical present and states, "My American life has been such a disappointment" (54).

As No Name Woman or the narrator of "The Yellow Wallpaper" illustrates, the constraints of motherhood may lead to madness, suicide, and death. In contrast, Kingston and Gilman seem able to envision ideal motherhood only within contexts that exceed or transcend normal limitations. Fa Mu Lan and the women of *Herland* do not need to master the maternal house, for they have done away with the house entirely. Gilman's utopian society does not adopt the concept of "home" and "family" while Fa Mu Lan leads a nomadic existence. Unfortunately, outside the realm of fantasy, there seems to be no way for a mother to avoid coming to terms with the maternal house and the cultural expectations of motherhood.

What all the autobiographies of mothers discussed in this chapter have in common is that they present only a partial view of a mother's experience. The mothers in this chapter were funny or very competent or completely incompetent or suicidal or insane or an idealization. This is not to say these representations of motherhood are inaccurate. Erma Bombeck's tremendously successful books are popular, in part, because much of what she writes about motherhood is true. The point is not that motherhood does not have its humorous moments but that it has other moments as well. These other moments—ones of anguish, frustration, depression, love, power, and powerlessness—might lack an audience. Can a mother write her story without making altruism, humor, hyperbole, or hysteria the dominant mode? Do we want to read about a "mom" who deviates from our frozen picture of that person, as Alta describes her, who "wore aprons, had curled blue-grey hair, & made peanut butter cookies with fork marks up & down & also sideways" (29)?

In the past twenty years, autobiographies by mothers who break away from the extremes of saintly mother/funny mother/hysterical mother are beginning to emerge. These mothers tread previously unspeakable ground. Alta, Nancy Mairs, Jane Lazarre, Elizabeth Fox-Genovese, Anne Roiphe, and Kathryn Grody are mothers who write the story traditionally accorded only to the daughter's less defined, less confined, position. That story, one of sexuality, conflict, desire, bodily function, and ambiguity, was not what mothers were supposed to write about.

Making Room for Mommy: The *Tranche de Vie* Autobiographies of Contemporary Mothers

> "Goddam it, Benjamin," I said and smacked him on his arm, wishing I had acted like the other woman. I took Benjamin off to the side, put my hand gently on his shoulder, appearing maternal, and whispered, "If you hit one more fucking child I will smack you so hard you will be black and blue."
>
> —Jane Lazarre, *The Mother Knot*

The "slice of life" or realistic autobiographies that have been emerging by mothers in the past few years *are* recognizable by more than their use of the word "fuck." Yet, this diction does serve to immediately alert the reader that this mother's autobiography is not going to read like *Please Don't Eat the Daisies*. Nevertheless, confusion may occur.

I first saw Kathryn Grody's autobiography, *A Mom's Life*, at Harry W. Schwartz Children's Bookshop. Schwartz's children's store, which I had some time ago dubbed "Schwartz, Jr.," was at that time located two doors down from the "adult" Schwartz bookstore in an affluent suburban mall. The children's bookshop is geared toward upwardly mobile parents with uniformly above-average children. The bookstore is antiseptically wholesome, with its juvenile books tastefully displayed and carefully screened.

Grody's book was the focus of a Mother's Day display. Surrounding Grody's books were entry blanks for the children to write an essay describing why their mother was the best mother in the world. Grody's book, apparently representative of motherhood, was described as providing "the unique joys of motherhood . . . funny and jolly . . . provocative . . . a delight." The description on the book jacket depicted the book similarly: "It's a three-ring circus of sticky fingers, flying foods and creative clowning. It's ketchup on tuna fish and the perfect recipe for soap bubbles."

Kathryn Grody herself is pictured on the cover, holding toys and a kitchen appliance while sitting on a (sketched in) baby stroller. Grody's expression is a mixture of exhaustion and sardonic good-humor. When I bought the book, I expected a domestic autobiography in the style of Erma Bombeck.

By the time I reached the third page of Grody's book, I was laughing. Grody, describing her growing frustration with her baby's crying, writes:

> "please go to sleep, please go to sleep, please damn it, please go to sleep!" . . . . I would sit on the hallway floor outside his room, listening to these intense shrieks. *Waaaaahhhhhhhhh!* "Please God, let this stop." *Waaahhhhh!* "Shit. Fuck. Why are five minutes taking forever?" (14,15)

. . . Clearly, no one at the children's bookshop had previewed the book. Instead, literally judging the book by its cover, as I had also done, the book was selected because it looked harmless, just another funny mother story.

And popular mothers, as the success of Erma Bombeck's books tell us, are harmless. They provide a good-natured, self-effacing background for the other, more active members of the family. As a character in Martha Bergland's novel, *A Farm Under a Lake*, astutely observes, " . . . the last thing you want when you're a child is an interesting mother" (179). The notion of an "interesting mother" implies a woman with an ego, who might entertain ideas not directly related to the welfare of her family. In contrast, Jane Lazarre, in *The Mother Knot*, outlines Western culture's myth of a "good mother": "She is quietly strong, selflessly giving, undemanding, unambitious; she is receptive and intelligent in only a moderate, concrete way; she is of even temperament, almost always in control of her emotions. She loves her children completely and unambivalently" (viii).

Even more threatening, perhaps, is the determination of interesting mothers like Jane Lazarre or Nancy Mairs to explore the maternal house, to examine their fears and their body. Previously, Mairs explains (quoting Hélène Cixous in part) women were alienated from themselves, from their own bodies: " 'Women haven't had eyes for themselves. They haven't gone exploring in their house. Their sex still frightens them. Their bodies, which they haven't dared enjoy, have been colonized.' Through writing her body, woman may reclaim the deed to her dwelling" (*Bone House* 7).

The mothers in recent autobiographies refuse to be "colonized," however, and have demonstrated that what is really frightening is a sexual, active mother with complex, ambivalent emotions. After all, if a mother is not in charge, then who is? Maybe no one, Kathryn Grody suggests. Mothers, Grody tells us, are often not in control—despite what Shirley Jackson would have us believe—and are scared as hell:

> This brings me to the subject of fears since becoming a mother. Did all moms always have these . . . . Were any times more innocent really, or is it the territory that comes with the awesomeness of the responsibility of being a mom? I'm afraid of dying young. I'm afraid of not seeing my children turn thirty. I'm afraid of the air becoming

unbreathable, afraid of the sun becoming unbathable, afraid of drunk
drivers, *afraid* . . . . (emphasis added, 20)

Though these mothers express their fears, they are not afraid to
write against the grain of the motherhood myth. Alta, for example, in her
autobiographical work, *Momma: a start on all the untold stories*, sati-
rizes Western culture's double movement of canonizing motherhood
while at the same time denigrating the American housewife: "people hate
housewives. youve probably noticed. jokes about us: we couldnt have
any brains or we wouldnt be doing this. & the women themselves (who
the hell do i think i am? *our*selves—) say "o, i'm just a housewife" (30).
Mothers, Alta suggests, may be worshipped in general but are somewhat
beneath consideration at a level of specificity, i.e., at the level of a
housewife:

> people from cities constantly ask me how i can stand to live in the
> suburbs where there is no one but housewives. & everyone knows
> housewives watch *as the world turns* (yes, i do) & talk about recipes.
> well youd be amazed. every woman here has a life. someday there
> will be a massive jail break & youll get to meet her for yourself. (31)

Alta realizes, however, that getting to "meet" the housewife for themselves is precisely what people do not want. Ideally, the housewife
should remain docile and invisible. Paradoxically, the culturally correct
housewife acts less like a mother than a (father's) daughter. Jaquie
Davison promotes the notion of an acquiescent, dependent wife and
mother in *I Am a Housewife!* (1972)—a book that is a unique combination of autobiography and self-help guide. The ideal housewife, Davison
tells us, acts like her daughter:

> Take a tip from your little daughter. Watch her uninhibited technique
> as she handles the man in her life, her father, your husband . . . . She
> obeys him without question: she gives him unstinted devotion. When
> he arrives home she runs, screaming with pleasure to throw her arms

around him, to hug and kiss him. When he tells her stories, no matter
how tall they are, she listens with wide-eyed interest and innocence.
She asks questions constantly so he can show off his intelligence . . .
(32)

Though Davison—depressingly—writes in complete earnest, her advice
echoes Virginia Woolf's highly ironic description of a woman's function: "Women have served all these centuries as looking glasses possessing the magic and delicious power of reflecting the figure of man at
twice its natural size" (35). Implicit, then, in Davison's description of a
successful housewife is the necessity for a woman to act like an infant
and thus magnify the importance of her husband (and children). It is a
schizoid performance, however, since on one level a woman should be-
have like her daughter and shower her husband with devotion while on
another she is highly conscious of using manipulation and "technique."

    In an another passage, Davison again explains the merits of a
housewife's demotion to infant status. Further, although Davison is apparently aware that housewives are being commodified by our culture,
she lauds the wisdom of the advertising industry nevertheless:

> I was walking through a department store and I saw some female
> sleeping apparel, and it was called a "baby doll". In other words,
> here are grown women, when the weather's warm, sleeping in some-
> thing called "baby dolls." What's more, the manufacturers are smart
> enough to give them names like that, knowing they won't be shunned.
> What does this mean? It means that women really like to be feminine
> and like to be baby dolls, protected, cared for, pampered. They want
> someone to take care of them. They don't want to be in charge. (33)

Or, perhaps what Davison is really identifying are the needs of our
society rather than the needs of a housewife. Since, by Davison's own
admission, a woman acting like a baby is a performance, her book may
tell us more about the desires of a culture than those of a housewife.
Though Davison paints an extreme picture of a submissive housewife,

she accurately reflects a culture that needs to subdue and infantilize motherhood. A woman following Davison's advice learns to bow to the desires of a dominant culture, since her own desires must be effaced and controlled to please her "man" and her children.

However, like so many of the critiques of wives and mothers, Davison's commentary lacks a socioeconomic base. Her exhortation for women to stay at home where they belong presumes a husband able to support a family and does not take into account the needs of divorced mothers, lesbian mothers, mothers with unemployed husbands, widowed mothers, mothers on welfare, etc. In America, Davison blithely argues, women are lucky because we have inherited the traditions of the "Age of Chivalry': "In America, a man's first significant purchase is a diamond for his bride, and the largest financial investment of his life is a home for her to live in. American husbands work hours of overtime to buy a fur piece or other finery to keep their wives in fashion . . . ." (77). Davison's description of the great good fortune of American women really applies to very few women.

Conversely, Alta foregrounds the social and economic factors that affect women. Her autobiography is a constant reminder that a woman's ability to write is predicated on privilege. For Alta, much like Virginia Woolf, privilege translates into (some) money and a room of one's own. Unlike Woolf, however, Alta's position as a mother makes her "room" prey to the constant invasion of her two young daughters. Alta writes starkly, with no irony, of her lack of time due to being a mother:

> if the baby coughs, this paragraph will end) & altho this story, this very story that i am writing, that of being a mother, is going on, i have not had the chance to tell it. *that is why our story has not been told.* we can either live it or write it, we cannot do both simultaneously. & no one can write it who has not lived it. (37)

Though Woolf, in *A Room of One's Own*, periodically discusses the difficulties brought on by motherhood, as a non-mother, she necessarily speaks at the level of theory. For Woolf, the alliance of writing and motherhood may not just be difficult but impossible. Woolf repeatedly portrays the presence of children in a woman's life as tragic and her imagined "Judith" Shakespeare commits suicide when she becomes pregnant. Alta, writing in the midst of motherhood, sees her life as intensely demanding rather than tragic. In large measure and in very real terms, Alta's autobiography serves to dramatize the halting, hurried process of a mother who writes.

Typographically, Alta's lack of capitalization, use of ampersands, and unusual punctuation attempt to mimic her own harried and chaotic existence. Norrine Voss, commenting similarly, notes that "since her [Alta's] life is cyclical and prone to interruption, her segmented, disorderly form perfectly embodies the reality of her life" and then quotes from Alta's book: "retyping this, i stopped to read the rest of this section & forgot to put the pages in order. so they are no longer in the same order i wrote them. in order, as if my life were in order. who am I kidding" (221). However much Alta's style of writing may appear to be merely an unconscious flow of language, a type of *écriture féminine*, Voss cautions that the reader should not mistake her method for an "inartistic, literal copy of her life" as she has still carefully "shaped her material" (222).

In style as well as content, then, Alta works to show the immense obstacles a woman with children and without money must overcome in order to write. Being a woman and a mother is the subject of Alta's autobiography. Defiantly, Alta's project stands in direct opposition to Woolf's caveat:

> it is fatal for any one who writes to think of their sex . . . . It is fatal for a woman to lay the least stress on any grievance; to plead even with justice any cause; in any way to speak consciously as a woman. And fatal is no figure of speech; for anything written with that conscious bias is doomed to death. It ceases to be fertilised. (108)

Paradoxically, though Woolf uses the metaphor of fertilization, her advice for a writer to adopt an androgynous stance explicitly effaces the position of woman and mother. For Woolf, the maternal house would best be ignored.

Conversely, what marks autobiographers like Nancy Mairs or Jane Lazarre is their determination to explore and articulate the maternal house—to define a woman's position as mother and body. Exploring the house as body—a blend of being that is both "wood and plaster and glass" as well as "bone and blood" (24) becomes the operative metaphor for Mairs' book, *Remembering the Bone House*. Mairs' subtitle, "An Erotics of Space and Place" also describes her intention to intimately map the rooms of her body, a body she views as unabashedly erotic:

> I mention my body, certainly quite a lot, even its secret places. Here and there I kiss, stroke, press, squeeze, even engage in sexual intercourse. Not as often, though, as I lie in bed, run across a playground, eat favorite foods, listen to the radio, tease my sister, roll in new snow. All these acts, happening to me as a body, shaping my new awareness of my embodied self, form my erotic being. It is that process I'm seeking to capture and comprehend: how living itself takes on an erotic tone. (8)

Domestic autobiographers such as Kerr or Bombeck deliberately ironize their relation to the maternal house, to their bodies. Kerr or Bombeck opt for the safer position of daughter (Interim Mother) and—when they discuss their bodies at all—speak ironically of their bodies' inadequacies, e.g., how clumsy their bodies are or how they are unable to improve their bodies by staying on a diet. The narrator of "The Yellow Wallpaper" becomes completely absorbed by the maternal house and loses her sanity while the women of *Herland* and the woman warrior, Fa Mu Lan, transcend the maternal house entirely.

Mairs, Lazarre, Alta, and, to a lesser degree, Grody confront the challenges of motherhood head on. Significantly, they direct their irony outward rather than inward. Alta *et al.* do not mock their bodies or their

position as mothers. Lazarre, for example, writes honestly—not humorously—about the changes pregnancy wreaks on her body:

> when I looked into that mirror at the foot of our bed and saw my na-
> ked body next to James, my vaginal canal suddenly felt as dry as an
> old sponge forgotten under the sink for months. I couldn't believe the
> sight of myself, belly protruding and breasts huger than they had ever
> been with nipples which suddenly doubled their size. No one ever
> told me to expect such things. I was outraged. (20)

For Lazarre, pregnancy becomes an invasion and her body has been
taken over by its immense physical changes. Similarly, Mairs' life has
also been invaded. Mairs describes the sensation of maternal love—not
as the exalted emotion we have been taught is normal but in its choking,
complicated reality:

> This love is wholly other than I expected. I was waiting for some
> surge, a tidal wave of maternal adoration, the sort of suffusing emo-
> tion you see depicted on the faces of all those Renaissance madonnas
> painted by men like Bellini and Carvaggio. This love doesn't over-
> whelm me. It undermines me, gets me from below, as though I were
> a tree, and Anne were another tree, whose roots put out tendrils there,
> out of sight. I'm suspended, sustained, in a vegetable tangle. A
> thicket of love. ("Bone House" 198)

For Mairs, the love her daughter arouses becomes a kind of trap; Mairs
feels sucked in and undermined by the relentless pull motherhood exerts.
     However, unlike the "slice of life" autobiographies of Lazarre or
Mairs, some of the more candid, more serious, mother autobiographies
also focus on the joyous aspects of mothering. Anne Roiphe, in her book
Fruitful: Living the Contradictions, A Memoir of Modern Motherhood
(1997) creates a work that is a combination of autobiography and feminist reassessment. While Mairs, and to a greater degree Lazarre, often
focus on motherhood's relentless toll in statements such as "Now I'm a

mother and that means I am nothing" (Lazarre qtd. in Roiphe 26), Roiphe dares to take feminists to task for ignoring the *positive* rewards of motherhood.

Though Roiphe is a feminist herself—and includes her own actions in her collective rebuke—she feels feminism "missed the boat" by consistently privileging more alternative lifestyles over motherhood. Instead of addressing motherhood politically and trying to come to terms with its complexity, motherhood became a dirty secret—just another thing women did to perpetuate "patriarchy." Roiphe tells how in the early days of the feminist movement just thinking about the power women now had made them feel like "Wonder Women with magic bracelets" but that when they focused on their roles as mothers, they felt embarrassed:

> When we thought of ourselves pushing strollers, dropping pieces of Lego across the living room floor, rushing home to give a sick child Tylenol, we just let it go, let the mothering side of ourselves become silent, almost as if we were ashamed of ourselves as nurturers, as protectors of the young. We suffered our maternal guilt house by house, woman by woman, the old-fashioned way. (113)

In spite of the fact that Roiphe also cites the pitfalls of motherhood: it can be boring, you often have to give up or defer your own desires for the "needs of a helpless, hapless human being," and you are at odds with feminism's insistence on "attention being paid to the self"; paradoxically, Roiphe concludes this section entitled "Motherhood: Gasp! No, Never, Not Me" by stating emphatically, "Nevertheless I still wanted more children" (29). Unfashionably, Roiphe finds herself identifying with Adèle Ratignolle who is the "mother-woman" foil to Edna Pontellier, the feminist heroine in Kate Chopin's *The Awakening*, and also finds herself impatient with Charlotte Perkins Gilman's tunnel vision in *Herland*:

> *Herland* is one of these visions that assumes an inherent difference in
> male and female character and capacity and make everything of it.
> Read as a corrective to male arrogance it's a wonderful fable. Read
> as a map of our predetermined nature it becomes a fairy tale. It's not
> completely untrue, it's just not all there is. Everyone who has ever
> been in a girls' school, on a girls' basketball team, within a female
> organization knows that women are not without aggression, competi-
> tion, cruelty, or hierarchies. (122)

In short, Roiphe argues that many feminists theorize or ignore motherhood rather than examining its realities. Mothers, whether they are "in-
vited" or not, factor heavily in the ongoing feminist debate. For feminism to grow and be relevant to all women—not just an elite few—
Roiphe argues that the emotions both "good and bad of the real mothers"
need to be understood (206). Further, Roiphe urges that feminism's
emphasis on a woman's self-fulfillment and a reasonable amount of self-
sacrifice need not be at odds: "Feminism, which was all about self-
fulfillment, forgot that giving up some of the self, which is necessary for
motherhood, is part of most women's self-fulfillment, another one of
God's not so funny jokes" (206).

Elizabeth Fox-Genovese in her book *Feminism Is not the Story of
My Life: How Today's Feminist Elite Has Lost Touch with the Real Concerns of Women* (1996)—as the subtitle suggests—focuses on many of
the issues articulated in Roiphe's autobiography. Defiantly, even the
cover designs serve to announce the two books' difference (from other
academic feminist works). Both the cover design on Fox-Genovese's
book and the original cover of Roiphe's book (published by Houghton-
Mifflin in 1996) foreground maternity. Fox-Genovese's book cover displays a mother closely embracing her young daughter while Roiphe's
cover design is dominated by the image of a baby viewed from the back;
most of the mother's image is obscured since the mother is holding the
baby in front of her. Clearly, both cover designs function to illustrate the
a child's significance in a mother's life.

Like Roiphe, Fox-Genovese begins her book by explaining her life in terms of the feminist movements and ideas emerging during and following her graduation from college in the early 1960s. Fox-Genovese tells how she works for the passage of the Equal Rights Amendment in the late 1960s and helps organize and faithfully attends a consciousness-raising group in the 1970s. Yet, as feminism evolves Fox-Genovese increasingly begins to realize that many of its beliefs do not address issues of motherhood and family central to her life and the lives of the numerous women of different race, class, and background that Fox-Genovese knows or interviews. Too often, she concludes, feminism only appears to represent all women. In a passage where Fox-Genovese specifically cites Susan Faludi, her criticism of Faludi's tactics could also apply to the general faults Fox-Genovese finds in much of feminism's ideology:

> Faludi claims to be writing for all women, but she focuses on the experience of those young single women in business and the professions who earn enough to support themselves in at least modest comfort and lead the lives they choose. She is not talking about women who can barely earn enough to support themselves, much less provide for children. Inadvertently, she leaves by the wayside women who might prefer—or feel a responsibility—to stay home while their children are young. What, we may ask, of the lives of the majority of women—who are outside the ranks of business, the academy, and the professions? (29)

Ultimately, coining Betty Friedan's expression from *The Feminine Mystique*, Fox-Genovese states that for contemporary women the "problem that has no name" is children (228). Just what, Fox-Genovese implicitly asks, are women supposed to do with their children (besides not having any)? Fox-Genovese argues that feminism encourages women to be free and fulfilled but refuses to acknowledge that often children, rather than men, "restrict women's independence," and it is children who "tend to make and keep a woman poor" (228). Fox-Genovese may be taking men out of this equation a little too precipitously. Nevertheless, she voices an articulate concern when she goes on to explain that few feminists "have been willing to state openly that women's freedom requires their freedom from children" (228). However, *whatever* a woman opts to do with her children is likely to arouse criticism. Paradoxically, Fox-Genovese asserts that "conservatives, who want mothers to stay home with their children, want welfare mothers to work, and feminists, who want most mothers to work, want welfare mothers to be able to stay home with their children" (238). Like Roiphe, Fox-Genovese sees that in order to thrive as a viable choice—for any woman—the work of mothering must be respected. Instead, Fox-Genovese finds that the feminists who seek to "free" women from mothering as well as the conservatives who want force women to stay home with their children "implicitly treat mothering as servants' work" (256). For Fox-Genovese, the solution will come only if feminism addresses the concerns of mothers, children, and family more clearly and by a "double attack" on society that would respect women's "needs and sensibilities" whether they choose to work outside the home or not (251).

Roiphe and Fox-Genovese, whose books are a mixture of autobiography and theory, do not denounce feminism so much as they ask that it re-examine, re-assess, and modify its theorizations about mothers. Though both Roiphe and Fox-Genovese acknowledge that mothering is hard—and often even boring—they stress the fact that mothering can also be intensely fulfilling.

While the ideas of Roiphe and Fox-Genovese may affront some feminists, the "slice of life" autobiographies—for lack of a more elegant term—of Alta, Lazarre, and Mairs may make readers in general uncomfortable. We are not used to reading about mothers who admit to resenting and even abusing their children, who foreground their sexuality and explain the many ways their husbands fail them as childrearing partners. Alta, Lazarre, and Mairs are often uncomfortable as well. Frequently, they question whether they are "normal" mothers and their tone—sometimes guilty, sometimes hesitant—demonstrates none of the

jovial ease of Bombeck who writes her mainstream accounts of motherhood with the support of an approving culture.

Clearly, all of these women—Alta, Lazarre, or Mairs—deviate from
the expectations of the motherhood myth, e.g., the 1950s and 1960s media parade of Donna Reed [*The Donna Reed Show*], Jane Wyatt [*Father
Knows Best*], Barbara Billingsley [*Leave It to Beaver*], Harriet Nelson
[*Ozzie and Harriet*], or Florence Henderson [*The Brady Bunch*]. Alta
writes of her experiences on welfare, her male lovers of various ethnici-
ties, and her lesbian relationship. Jane Lazarre marries an African-
American man and describes the added difficulty they encounter trying
to find a child care center they could both afford and that would offer a
racial mix for their son. Nancy Mairs depicts her extramarital affairs and
the growing frustration she feels as her multiple sclerosis interferes with
her life. Kathryn Grody's book—an uneasy combination of candid despair and Bombeck humor—comes the closest to forming a bridge between the domestic autobiographies and the "slice of life" writings.

Alta's book—little discussed and little known—was published by a
non-profit press. This new genre of frank accounts of motherhood may
not, as yet, even have an audience. The problem is partly one of space; a
mother who takes as well as gives, might get in our way. To perpetuate
the Oedipal ideology, a mother's desire must be silent, as Marianne
Hirsch explains: "Within a psychoanalytic framework, the mother's
desire can never be voiced because her desire exists only in the fantasy
of the child as something the child can never satisfy" (168). An actively
desiring mother—and this includes the simple desire "to be" as well as
sexual desires—who represents herself as subject rather than as her
husband's or children's object, thus upsets the familial apple cart. At
present, there may not even be room for a mother who refuses to stay in
the background. Without new theories of motherhood—written by both
daughters and mothers—mothers will remain a cultural metaphor, the
locus of passivity, selflessness, and invisibility.

V

Conclusion: Mother, Body, and Metaphor

... woman, if I have read correctly, never appears at any point along
the umbilical cord, either to study or to teach .... No woman or trace
of woman, if I have read correctly—save the mother, that's understood. But this is part of the system. The mother is the faceless figure of a *figurant*, an extra. She gives rise to all the figures by losing
herself in the background of the scene like an anonymous persona.
Everything comes back to her, beginning with life; everything addresses and destines itself to her. She survives on condition of remaining at bottom.

—Jacques Derrida, *The Ear of the Other*

The Site of Motherhood Revisited

This book examines how women textually represent their mothers or
themselves as mothers in autobiography. It could also be described, to
borrow words from Nancy K. Miller and Adrienne Rich, as a poetics and
politics of location, in this case, of the location of motherhood.

In the first chapter, the autobiographical process was linked to allegory. Like allegory, autobiography's narrative structure highlights and
spatializes certain moments. To use de Man's terms, perception itself is
allegorical, always an operation of "blindness and insight." In much of
women's life-writing, a daughter's "insight" pivots on her own mind and
her mother's body. The consequent invisible space—the site of blindness—becomes the daughter's body and her mother's mind. Mary
McCarthy makes the mind/body dichotomy patently clear in the opening
to her autobiography, *How I Grew*:

> I was born as a mind during 1925, my bodily birth having taken place
> in 1912. Throughout the thirteen years in between, obviously, I must
> have had thoughts and mental impressions, perhaps even some sort of
> specifically cerebral life that I no longer remember. Almost from the
> beginning, I had been aware of myself as "bright." (1)

In keeping with the generic prescriptions of autobiography,
McCarthy quickly dissociates from her body—following her "bodily
birth"—and limns her life in terms of her mind. Like Beauvoir, McCarthy foregrounds her mind, afraid to be perceived as a body. Her fear, as
Adrienne Rich explains, re-enacts the mind/body cultural trap to which
women have long been prey. In some instances, women simply give into
the trap and become "bodies—blindly, slavishly, in obedience to male
theories about [them]" (Rich 285). Other women, in an attempt to be
perceived as intellectual, have opted to deny the body altogether:

> "I don't *want* to be the Venus of Willendorf—or the eternal fucking
> machine." Many women see any appeal to the physical as a denial of
> mind. We have been perceived for too many centuries as pure Na-
> ture, exploited and raped like the earth and the solar system; small
> wonder if we now long to become Culture: pure spirit, mind. (285)

While it is unfortunate is that women have often felt the need to choose
between their minds and their bodies, since we are always *both*, a mother
might not even have *this* choice. No one is perceived as "pure Nature"
more markedly than mothers; the maternal body cannot be denied. As
Marianne Hirsch comments, "the figure of the mother is determined by
her body more intensely than the figure of woman" (12).

In an essay entitled "Of Other Spaces," Michel Foucault describes a
space he calls a "heterotopia," a "counter-site," a "placeless place." As
examples, Foucault mentions places like cemeteries or junkyards—often
situated in out-of-way spots—that we drive by and literally do not see.
The reflection a mirror provides also functions like a placeless place; we
see ourselves in some other place, a heterotopia: "In the mirror, I can see

myself there where I am not, in an unreal, virtual space that opens up behind the surface; I am over there, there where I am not, a sort of shadow that gives my own visibility to myself " (24). The mirror, then, operates like an invisible medium able only to reflect other surfaces.

Traditionally, a mother functions like this mirror, able to reflect the images of the other, more active members of the family (i.e., father, son, and daughter) by maintaining her position in a non-space. As Dana Heller notes (quoting Andrea Press in passing), the television media have helped to reinforce this view. Heller describes the opening scene of *The Donna Reed Show*, where everything the mother (Donna Reed) does "during the brief sequence is determined by the needs and desire of her husband and children" (47). Further, Heller comments that there is "nothing unusual about this, as Press observes that early television mothers are 'rarely (if ever) . . . shown to be mature independent individuals . . . . [They] are consistently pictured almost exclusively in the domestic or private realm" (47–48). Or—to put this more succinctly— traditionally, a mother exists to serve others. A mother who would *instead* focus her reflective planes inward to see herself, to consider her own desires, literally has to create space for herself within our existing family structures.

For many daughters as autobiographers, however, the mother has merely functioned as a useful reflective surface. The mother provides a body that the daughter may safely dissect and desire while keeping her own representation carefully entrenched in cultural space. And this is not always a conscious process. Often, the mother operates as a blind spot for daughters. I could not "see," for example, how persistently mothers were absent or relegated to body by both male and female writers of fiction, autobiography, and theory, until I became a mother myself. After becoming a mother, I listened with astonishment as people made comments about "Earth Mothers" and maternal instincts, amazed that no one would have considered making the same type of generalizations about daughters, sons, or fathers. Apparently, it was not evident that making assumptions about mothers as if they were all in one, changeless category effected a massive erasure.

As a daughter, however, I would have made the same comments, assuming—on some disinterested level—that mothers were pretty much the same. Like Adrienne Rich, I looked at my mother and thought that "I too shall marry, have children—but *not like her*. I shall find a way of doing it all differently" (219). I worked to keep my identity distinct from my mother's, even if it meant erasing my mother's identity in the process . . .

The Dis-Location of Maternal Space

I think I longed to . . . get free of Mama. My skin crawled with her. She was everywhere, all over me, inside and out. Her influence clung, membrane-like, to my nostrils, my eyelids, my open mouth. I drew her into me with every breath I took. I drowsed in her etherizing atmosphere, could not escape the rich and claustrophobic character of her presence, her being, her suffocating, suffering femaleness.

—Vivian Gornick, *Fierce Attachments*

I always had nightmares. When I was a teenager, I used to dream that I was being strangled by another woman and, at other times, that I was strangling her. Though the dream's dynamics of aggression switched back and forth, always there was murderous intent. It was only after I had had the dream for some time that I woke one morning and, remembering the dream more vividly, suddenly realized the other woman was my mother. After I had my own children, I no longer had the dream. Apparently, I was letting go of the old resentments. I am not sure why. Perhaps I now realized—as a mother—how difficult it was to ever feel you were doing anything right, how difficult it must have been for my mother. Or maybe it was when I saw—or imagined—my children begin constructing their own narratives of recrimination.

For my daughter, as opposed to my sons, these narratives will only be more intense since I—as a woman and her mother—not only affect her future but predict her future as well. If I wrote my autobiography or my daughter wrote hers, we would both have to re-confront our mothers. A daughter who tries to write her story necessarily becomes entangled in her mother's story and places her own identity at risk.

Kim Chernin, whose mother asks that she write the story of their four generations of women (that of her grandmother, her mother, Chernin herself, and her own daughter), at first hesitates, knowing she chances being "consumed" (16) by undertaking this "enterprise":

> it is not easy to turn from the path I have imagined for myself. This enterprise will take years. It will draw me back into the family, waking its ghosts. It will bring the two of us [Chernin and her mother] together to face all the secrets and silences we have kept. The very idea of it changes me. I'm afraid. I fear, as any daughter would, losing myself back into the mother. (12)

Chernin's fear echoes that of Irigaray's speaker in "And the One Doesn't Stir Without the Other" who pleads with her mother: "You put yourself in my mouth, and I suffocate . . . . Continue to be also outside. Keep yourself/me outside. Don't be engulfed, don't engulf me, in what passes from you to me. I would so much like that we both be here. That the one does not disappear into the other or the other into the one" (qtd. in Gallop 114).

What Irigaray and Chernin both articulate is a fear of maternal margins and boundaries: Will I become my mother? Will my mother become me? Will I know the difference? And, perhaps most importantly, because these women write for an audience: Will people confuse me with my mother? Most of the daughters *and* mothers discussed in the preceding chapters train an anxious eye on the margin between mother and daughter. Simone de Beauvoir, in a gesture familiar among autobiographical daughters, carefully aligns herself with her father—the

site of intellect and logos—after paying brief homage to her mother's
beauty. Conversely, daughters such as Nathalie Sarraute actively desire
their mothers and—if anything—appear to want to break down the
barrier between mother and daughter altogether. Yet, the mother Sarraute desires, and obsessively presents in her text, is only an erotic surface, all body and touch. Annie Dillard, who sets out to prove her
mother's unusual (i.e., different/better than "other" mothers) intellect and
wit, cannot help returning over and over to her mother's body. Dillard—
caught in the values of a conformist society—repeatedly reveals her
pride in her mother's culturally correct body: slim, blond, and tan.

Nancy Friday, whose autobiography, *My Mother/My Self*, ostensibly
foregrounds her mother as subject, ultimately feels no assurance that her
autobiography is not just another lie she and her mother share. Her textual representation of her mother—a metaphorical birth—is also, and
perhaps always in any autobiographical work, an act of execution as
well. Barbara Johnson, writing on Friday's autobiography, comments
similarly: "How, then can we be sure that this huge book is not itself another lie to the mother it is dedicated to? Is autobiography somehow always in the process of symbolically killing the mother by telling her the
lie that we have given birth to ourselves?" (147). As Johnson suggests,
an autobiography that follows the traditional trajectory of autonomy will
always threaten, if not directly efface, the mother's importance.

Even mothers themselves, as may be evidenced in the domestic
autobiographies of Erma Bombeck, Shirley Jackson, or Jean Kerr, often
devise ways to maintain a distance from the site of motherhood. Motherhood, evidently, is a negatively charged space, a location that must be
idealized and dismissed, avoided altogether, reduced to a cultural metaphor, or completely transcended. The fear that occupying the maternal
position evokes might be suggested by indirection.

As I wrote this book, a friend of mine was reading it as I went
along. Repeatedly, she advised me to put more of myself in my writing.
When she said, "Write in your own voice," what she was really asking
was that I speak as a mother. It was the hardest writing that I have ever

done. Every time I wrote as a mother, I felt inauthentic, unscholarly, and vulnerable. In particular, I felt alone. I could not lean comfortably back on the shoulders of academe and dredge up innumerable quotes to support my position because there weren't any (. . . or very few). In fact, I found it slightly ironic that after many years of carefully effacing my position as a mother, my most extended work foregrounded that very fact.

To write this book, then, I had to relocate myself. Like most mothers in academics, I had learned to dislocate the maternal from my speech and my writing. Adrienne Rich, whose eloquent work, *Of Woman Born*, is a blend of autobiography and cultural criticism, similarly describes her initial difficulties in writing the book in other than the traditional academic mode:

> It seemed to me impossible from the first to write a book of this kind without being often autobiographical, without often saying 'I.' Yet for many months I buried my head in historical research and analysis in order to delay or prepare the way for the plunge into areas of my own life which were painful or problematical. (15–16)

Surprisingly, this maternal avoidance occurs in the midst of a resurgence of theorization on motherhood. For the past twenty years, both American and Continental theorists have been writing on motherhood. Few academics, though, dare to write from the mother's position, possibly fearing the reception Julia Kristeva received in the "motherly/semiotic" portion of "Stabat Mater." Significantly, then, the theories on motherhood originate largely *from* the daughter's position and *about* the mother's body. The metaphorization of the mother's body—whether maternity is presented as a positive or a negative value—may, ultimately, leave mothers in the same position.

The Economy of *Écriture Féminine*

No object is in a constant relationship with pleasure (Lacan, apropos of Sade).

For the writer, however, this object exists: it is not the language, it is the mother tongue. The writer is someone who plays with his mother's body . . . in order to glorify it, to embellish it, or in order to take it to the limit of what can be known about the body . . .

—Roland Barthes, *The Pleasure of the Text*

Articles such as Ann Rosalind Jones', "Writing the Body: Toward an Understanding of *L'Écriture Féminine*," Susan Rubin Suleiman's, "Writing and Motherhood," and Domna C. Stanton's, "Difference on Trial: A Critique of the Maternal Metaphor in Cixous, Irigaray and Kristeva," Marianne Hirsch's book, *The Mother/Daughter Plot*, as well as Michelle Boulous Walker's recent book, *Philosophy and the Maternal Body* (1998), may provide a summary of the dominant critical theory on motherhood, the mother's body, and its relation to language. Suleiman, Stanton, and Hirsch begin by first reviewing previous—largely male—psychoanalytic theories of motherhood. Cixous's introduction to her essay, "Sorties: Out and Out: Attacks/Ways Out/Forays" could serve as an overview of the position of woman—and particularly the position of "mother"—in Western culture:

> Where is she?
>
> > Activity/Passivity
> > Sun/Moon
> > Culture/Nature
> > Day/Night
> > Father/Mother . . . woman is always associated with passivity in philosophy . . . . Intention: desire, authority—examine them and you are led right back . . . to the father. Ultimately the world of "being" can function while precluding the mother. No need for a mother, as long as there is some motherliness: and it is the father, then, who acts the part, who is the mother. Ei-

> ther woman is passive or she does not exist.
> What is left of her is unthinkable, unthought.
> (559, 561)

Motherhood, in this theorization, is intrinsically negative, literally *the* negation of culture, intention, and productivity.

In contrast, Stanton explains how Cixous, Irigaray, and Kristeva advocate a "valorization of the maternal" by reversing the values inherent in traditional binary codification (160). To simplify (there are important differences in the arguments of Cixous, Irigaray, and Kristeva), they shift the positive value to the right side of the binary. In this theorization, nature, fluidity, intuition, otherness, and the pre-Oedipal are not only celebrated but also seen as the site of production, language, and artistic creation.

The celebratory gesture of the French feminists may be less innovative than it would first appear. Motherhood has long been linked to artistic creation, even if she (the mother) has only been used a blank canvas. Suleiman, correspondingly, explains how in "Melanie Klein's theory of artistic creation, the mother—or rather, the mother's body— functions as a 'beautiful land' to be explored" (357). The mother, then, serves as an impetus to creative production; as a "body" the artist seeks "to appropriate, the thing he loses or destroys again and again, and seeks to recreate" (Suleiman 360). In short, the mother's body may inspire creativity but the mother herself is passive and (verbally) uncreative; she does not write.

Ostensibly, Hélène Cixous appears to link writing to motherhood directly. Cixous depicts the relation between women, mothers, and language in the "The Laugh of the Medusa":

> Even if phallic mystification has generally contaminated good relationships, a woman is never far from "mother" (I mean outside her role functions: the "mother" as nonname and as source of goods). There is always within her at least a little of that good mother's milk. She writes in white ink. (312)

Cixous's use of the word "mother" is complex. She says in several instances that mother is "a metaphor" (312). In the passage quoted above,
certainly, it is not clear whether the "woman" *is* a mother herself or, instead, is able to tap into some kind of motherhood essence: "that good
mother's milk." Plainly, the use of the phrase, "mother's milk," is meta-
phoric and not entirely gender-bound. Cixous sees feminine writing
nearly absent in literary history (it is a writing, she posits, that has yet to
emerge) but does cite male writers such as Heinrich von Kleist and Jean
Genet as demonstrating traces of *écriture féminine*.

If male writers may also access the "mother's milk" and write in
"white ink," the mother's body, notwithstanding Cixous's disclaimer, has
once again become a "source of goods" (312). Michele Boulous Walker
finds Cixous's emphasis on the "breast" replicating some fairly familiar
masculine metaphors:

> To focus on the breast rather than the breasts is already to de-eroticize
> the mother's body reducing it to the site of nurturance. It is a way of
> ensuring the mother remains a mother only in relation to birth and
> suckling. There is something decidedly Oedipal lurking behind
> Cixous' celebratory manifesto of the mother. Her simple yet lyrical
> assertion that mothers must write themselves with the mother's white
> ink reduces both women and mother to stereotypically eroticised
> sites. (140)

And what of the "white ink"? Can it be discerned against the expanse of
white paper or will the milk—the mother's body—again fade into the
background, once more invisible, undecipherable, and othered.

Julia Kristeva similarly links the maternal body to artistic creation.
Stanton, summarizing Kristeva's position, explains that "Poetic language, art in general, is, then, 'the semiotization of the symbolic'" (166).
The semiotic, which Kristeva generally refers to as the semiotic *chora*,
originates from the maternal body: "The mother's body is therefore what
mediates the symbolic law organizing social relations and becomes the
ordering principle of the semiotic *chora*" (95). Kristeva's pre-Oedipal,

pre-symbolic female language of *jouissance* thus attains its initial drives and impetus from the mother's body. For a woman, Kristeva cautions, in "About Chinese Women," toying with the pre-Oedipal by responding to "the call of the mother" (156), is mortally threatening: "Once the moorings of the word, the ego, the superego, begin to slip, life itself can't hang on: death moves quietly in" (157). Kristeva, like Cixous, indicates that male writers—e.g., Joyce and Genet—have more safely, more successfully, produced "female" writing.

Irigaray links the mother's body to *écriture féminine* (or *jouissance* or *womenspeak*) far less specifically than Kristeva or Cixous. In fact, although Stanton's article directly critiques the use of the maternal metaphor in Kristeva, Cixous, and Irigaray, there is little corroboration in Irigaray's work that she foregrounds maternity at all. In evidence, Stanton cites Irigaray's frequent description of feminine language as being fluid, multiple, and open. Stanton posits that Irigaray, like Cixous, "consistently exploits the age-old association of mother and water" (169).

More often, however, Irigaray frames her descriptions of *jouissance* within a "woman's" libidinal economy and, for Irigaray, the words "woman" and "mother" appear to represent different poles. Gallop comments on Irigaray's pronounced woman/mother dichotomy in the beginning of her essay, "When Our Lips Speak Together," which calls for a new, purely female woman-to-woman speech and language:

> [Irigaray's essay] begins: 'If we continue to speak the same language to each other, we are going to reproduce the same history.' That text attempts not to repeat the same, rather to change, to make progress. But a parenthesis interrupts the lyrical flow, brusquely reminding the reader of a less idyllic, more familiar context: 'I love you, you who are neither mother (Excuse me Mother, I prefer a woman to you) nor sister.' (113)

As Gallop notes, Irigaray's parenthetical comment clearly organizes "mother" and "woman" into different categories. Further, Irigaray consistently links "woman" to the daughter's position, the position from which Irigaray speaks as well. Despite Irigaray's ostensibly fluid, libidinal economy—the imagery Stanton views as evoking the mother's body—Irigaray recurrently expresses a fear and distaste for the maternal position which she sees threatening her own autonomy as a daughter.

Somewhat whimsically, then, in her work, *The Daughter's Seduction*, Gallop stages a dialogue between Irigaray-the-daughter and Kristeva-the-mother. It is precisely Irigaray's determination to speak from the daughter's position, to actively avoid and fear the mother's location, Gallop posits, that empowers and phallicizes the mother (117). Further, Irigaray's assumption that there can even be mother/woman categories elides a great deal of the complexity in female relationships. Kristeva, as Gallop reminds us, theorizes that "the relation to the mother is always, in some way, reproduced between women" (116). Also, to deny that a daughter and mother inevitably overlap is to "naively believe" that a mother and daughter could ever be completely separate:

> It is to deny that one's mother is a woman, to deny any identification with one's mother. Certainly it is a stultifying reduction to subsume femininity into the category of maternity. But it is an opposite and perhaps even equally defensive reduction to believe in some simple separation of the two categories. (116)

Conversely, Kristeva's desire to speak from the mother's position, to name that previously unnamed and unspoken position, makes the mother more complex and less phallic. Like the *tranche de vie* autobiographers (Alta, Jane Lazarre, or Nancy Mairs) discussed in the previous chapter, Kristeva treads on forbidden ground. Yet, just as Alta's or Lazarre's desire to change and complicate Western civilization's assumptions of motherhood could gel into a new set of assumptions about motherhood, Kristeva must keep maternal boundaries and theorizations fluid or else risk phallicizing the very position she wishes to de-mystify.

Cixous, Irigaray, and Kristeva's theories all snag on the body of the mother. Part of the problem, Stanton suggests, is inherent in the process of metaphorization itself. A metaphor, which functions to fill in for a "missing term," "to name the unnamed," creates an inevitable re-distribution of power, e.g., the contents of container A may shift to container B but the containers and the mechanization of containment will remain the same:

> The problematic of the unrepresented is not peculiar to the maternal metaphor. It is endemic to any practice that tries to name the unnamed; it is embedded in the bind that all affirmation of difference creates. For either we name and become entrapped in the structures of the already named; or else we do not name and remain trapped in passivity, powerlessness, and a perpetuation of the same. (Stanton 164)

Cixous' use of the mother's milk (the white ink), Kristeva's semiotic chora, and Irigaray's reference to amniotic fluids all work to batten the mother's body for parts. Once again, the mother's body becomes the source—but not necessarily the producer—of artistic creation. To turn the mother's body into a metaphor—whether in the course of feminist theorization or not—is merely to replicate all the old gestures. What writers such as Lazarre, Alta, or Mairs (speaking from the mother's position) or Kim Chernin (speaking from both the daughter and mother's position) demonstrate is that we do not, as yet, even know what mothers are, what they have been, or what they could be.

In her essay, Stanton asks for an "offputting" of the maternal metaphor (177). More to the point, we might want to consider whether motherhood—and particularly the mother's body—should operate as a metaphor at all. As long as motherhood is reduced to a metaphor, that position—in any real sense—will remain marginal, possibly feared, and certainly disempowered. The mother's body—our imaginary site of the unknown, the dark, and the hidden—may be the most dominant metaphor of our culture. A postmodern parable—describing the re-configuration of family following organ transplantation—may serve to illustrate the pervasiveness of maternal displacement in our culture. Whatever we mortally fear, we cannot understand, and we cannot intellectually control, becomes (metaphorically) linked to the mother's body.

Epilogue:
Re-Membering, Re-Mothering the Postmodern Body

For the body is that which is situated as the precise opposite of the conceptual, the abstract. It represents the ultimate constraint on speculation or theorization, the place where the empirical finally and always makes itself felt . . . . Science fiction, a genre specific to an era of rapid technological development, frequently envisages a new, revised body as a direct outcome of the advance of science. And when technology intersects with the body in the realm of representation, the question of sexual difference is inevitably involved . . . . A certain anxiety concerning the technological is often allayed by a displacement of this anxiety onto the figure of the woman or the idea of the feminine.

—"Technophilia" Mary Ann Doane (163)

In a sense, autobiography could be viewed as a precursor to modern technology. Paul John Eakin, in fact, subtitles his work on autobiography, "Studies in the Art of Self-Invention." Self-invention, taken literally, presumes a God-like self who is the product of his/her own creation and who has thus bypassed the regular course of birth and nurturing. Technology similarly effaces biological beginnings, working instead to create a world capable of being controlled by intellect and not betrayed by the body. The mother's body—that reminder of our birth and guarantor of our eventual death—stands most at odds with technology and the autonomous drive of autobiography.

Mothering as Disease

Paradoxically, for Simone de Beauvoir, herself considered a "mother" of feminism, the concept of mother represents all that resides on the right side of the male/female binary. In this dualism, a dualism explored at length in the second chapter, mother equals passivity, nature, night, pathos, instinct, and body versus the father's attributes of activity, culture, day, logos, intellect, and mind. Everything that exceeds our intellectual control, that resists logic and order, resides in this conceptual chain: mother, nature, pathos, and body. In short, as "Bataille knew, and Cixous reminds us, the fear of the right side of the binary is the fear of death itself" (Latimer 558).

If the mother is conceptually linked to body, disease, and death, the changing configurations of the body's boundaries due to medical technology bear investigation. Vital organ transplantation, for example, which has rapidly escalated in the past fifteen years, changes our notion of what is and what is not part of our own bodies, as well as providing a means of at least deferring what were, in the past, death sentences. In other words, organ transplantation changes our concept of life as well as our concept of death. We may now become recipients of vital organs instead of dying or, conversely, we may donate our own organs and thus, in part, perpetuate ourselves after death. Organ transplantation also creates a new family dynamics that call into question the traditional positions of mother, father, and child.

A transplant recipient is both re-born—and thus, in a sense, re-mothered—as well as re-organized; the patient's body is not the same body that it was, and the patient's family is similarly changed and displaced. More than any other area of medicine, organ transplantation accomplishes what Mary Shelley first introduced: the "creation, continuation, variation, and destruction, of life" via "scientific, technological and intellectual" means (Spector 163). The position assigned to the mother in a transplant patient's reformulation of family highlights the process of mothering as metaphor and bears directly on the representation of women's bodies and how motherhood emerges as part of an ideological chain.

Further, as consumers, we apparently like reading about illness. Perversely, reading about illness allows us to "toy" with images of disease and death while keeping a safe distance. In an annotated bibliography of American autobiographies from 1945 to 1980, autobiographies of illnesses ranging from brain tumors to jungle rot constituted the largest subject category (Briscoe). Situated as it is, in some gray limbo between death and life, organ transplantation may be the most dramatic and the most ethically complicated area to develop in medicine in this century. It is, then, a future subject of autobiography destined to interest and to reach a large audience. How organ transplantation ultimately may alter the shape of autobiography as well as highlight the process of maternal displacement in our culture may be suggested by beginning with an autobiographical aside of my own.

Re-Organizing the Body

Some time ago while driving home, I listened to the news on the radio. A fourteen year-old boy had died of self-inflicted gunshot wounds. I thought of my own children and wondered how any parent could cope with a child's suicide. Almost immediately, I speculated on whether his organs would be donated and if the various transplant teams (heart, lung, kidney, liver, etc.) were at work determining how many organs could be used. Within seconds, my concept of the boy had changed from that of human being to that of product.

The tools and prosthetic devices of postmodern technology disorder our belief in the natural body. Our bodies are repaired and rebuilt, made cosmetically acceptable, and aided by artificial apparatus. Psychologically, however, there is a profound difference between a silicone implant or even an artificial heart and the implantation of a vital organ from another body. Transplantation disrupts the notion of bodily wholeness and unity, and the language of postmodern medical technology betrays this schism. An organ is assessed to determine if it may be "harvested" for "implantation," terminology evocative of agriculture and production. Conversely, the terminology describing the actual transference of organs from one body to another remains curiously polite, a transaction between "donor" and "host."

That evening, on the same day the boy died, my husband, a transplant cardiologist, returned home and said the boy had, in fact, been evaluated by the transplant teams. My husband had needed to get a history from the boy's parents. In transplantation, the history is less one of the patient—an entire human being—than that of the organ, in this case, the heart: any murmurs? rheumatic fever? chest pain? arrhythmias? The disconnected organ itself reveals ongoing narratives—diseases and infections that must be read to determine if they will conflict with the body of the host. When immunosuppressant drugs are given to the organ recipient to prevent rejection, the host's body suddenly spouts its own narratives. Shutting down the immune system literally awakens the body. The body begins to tell its own history; a trip to Mexico or France fifteen years ago may now yield a disease previously suppressed. When the donor organ and the immunosuppressed body of the recipient unite, their combined and conflicting narratives enact the intertextuality of the postmodern body with a vengeance. Roland Barthes, in his autobiography, comments on the (im)possibility of writing the body (180). How then will the multiple body, a body *literally* re-organized, be represented?

Death operates as the subtext of autobiography. Autobiography presumes a future rather than a contemporary audience, and its teleology makes death the controlling metaphor. Though other life stories—biographies and fictional *bildungsromane*—generally end with the character's actual death, death necessarily remains deferred in autobiography. While autobiographers cannot—logically—write their death, the trajectory of autobiography—i.e., the story of a person's birth, maturation, and growth makes the imminence of death an implicit part nonetheless. Further, as Peter Brooks has theorized, whether death is represented or not, readers will, nevertheless, desire and anticipate the "end":

> The sense of a beginning, then, must in some important way be determined by the sense of an ending. We might say that we are able to read present moments—in literature and, by extension, in life—as endowed with narrative meaning only because we read them in anticipation of the structuring power of these endings that will retrospectively give them the order and significance of plot. (94)

The dynamics of transplantation, however, disrupt endings, impede autobiography's directness, and perforate death's closure. After dying, our body may now become a site of production, enabling other bodies to survive, while, conversely, someone else's death may prolong our own bodies. Unlike other life-saving surgeries—however dramatic—vital organ transplantation differs in its inherent check and balance of life and death: someone must die for someone to live and, further, body parts must intersect. This intersection of bodies in life and death blurs death's boundaries as well as creating a new ethics of body relations.

Thomas Thompson, in his book, *Hearts*, provides an extreme example of bodily intersection. Speculating on full head transplants, Thompson writes—quite matter-of-factly:

> Not totally out of the realm of possibility is that entire heads might be transplanted some decade hence. Russian surgeons grafted the head of a dog onto another in 1954, and the animal lived briefly. If an entire human head were transplanted, the donor would, in effect, become the recipient, because his brain would be transplanted to another body. (143)

In Thompson's example not only are body parts exchanged but the dynamics of transplantation becomes reversed: the donor becomes the recipient. Thompson's example may seem bizarre or even repulsive but, as

A. C. Greene writes in the autobiography of his heart transplant (*Taking Heart*):

> We can be amused at the outlandish idea that the brain or the entire human head might be transposed, medically, but I am sure that if an archivist a century or so from now digs into some molding copies of this work, that twenty-first or twenty-second century archivist will be even more amused that we were bemused at the prospect . . . . Remember, our imaginations can seldom keep up with our inventions. (173)

A. C. Greene is right. It is hard to "imagine" how profoundly full body or full head transplants would affect one's subjectivity and, in turn, autobiography. Even with *internal* organ transplants the host may be deeply influenced by the gender or race of the donor organ. Internal organ transplanting may be done by heterografting (male to female or vice-versa) as well as trans-racially. A. C. Greene relates the story (from Lee Gutkind's book, *Many Sleepless Nights*) of a "male liver transplantee who received a woman's liver, and once out of the hospital, began introducing himself as being 'pieced together with my new wife'" (150). Greene also cites how the gender of the donor organ may initiate speculation on the part of the recipient: "'If I get a woman's heart, will I feel about sex like a woman? and vice-versa, or 'Wonder what kind of a guy the donor was sexually? or 'Will a stranger's heart affect my sex personality?'" (151). Clearly, organ transplantation effects psychological as well as physical change.

Transplant patients repeatedly speak of not being the same person. The theme of new life consistently surfaces in the dialogue of transplant patients who speak of being given "a second chance at life" and see their life, not as a continuation of their old life but as something new, as one patient explains when she says, "I get up in the morning and everything looks different . . . . When something little happens that would have upset me years ago, I'm not upset at all" (Bucior 6, 12). Though many "near-death" experiences might generate the same sort of response, A. C.

Greene argues that for transplant patients the change is radical and unanimous:

> One thing I have become convinced of from talking with dozens of transplantees is that the process leads to change, great change, without and within—especially within . . . . You are not the same, you do not have the same outlook on life or death . . . . You are changed by something medical science still can't put its gloved finger on . . . . The *you* you lived "before" seems to be someone else's life. (176)

The "new-ness" of transplant patients' lives via their figurative re-birth, also re-organizes their family dynamics and re-casts the central figures in the Oedipal drama: mother, father, and child. Who, for example, "mothers" the transplant recipient? If "mother," as a verb, means to "give birth" or "give life," the donated vital organ operates as a mother to a terminally ill patient. The patient, of course, becomes the child.

A hospital's depersonalization and infantilization of its patients has long been documented. One becomes, first of all, a body. If, as many specialists have argued, organ transplantation places more emotional stress on patients than any other medical procedure ("Psychopathology," Kuhn 224), all the effects of depersonalization and dependency increase exponentially. You are now defined as a *body*. A patient's reduction to body becomes dramatically evident in the book, *Heartsounds*, which is somewhat of a biography and autobiography combined, since it is written by the journalist, Martha Lear, about her husband, Dr. Harold Lear, who relates his feelings and impressions to Martha during the three years he is dying from heart disease. As a doctor, his perspective is particularly revealing; he understands medical protocol but now has the opportunity to experience this protocol as a patient. Martha Lear writes of his reactions when he is rushed into the emergency room suffering from a massive heart attack: "He understood that at this moment he was no more than a body with pathology. They were not treating a person; they were treating an acute coronary case in severe shock. They were racing, very quickly, against time. He himself had run this race so often, working in just this detached silent way on nameless, faceless bodies with pathologies" (7). And, again, Lear wryly describes his dual perspective just before he undergoes a heart catheterization:

> There was something schizoid here. It was all so familiar, yet so utterly strange. He had never been in such a setting lying down. He had always been one of those masked faces that floated way up there, in the semilight, peering down at bodies stretched on tables like this. So this is how it looks from the other side, he thought. A room with a different view. Worm's eye views. Infants in their cradles gazing up at giants. (126)

Transplant patients' altered view of their lives may be evidenced by the manner in which they construct their autobiographies. Their life-stories begin with a description of the end-stage disease, work through the various stages of organ transplant protocol, and end with a description of their "new" life. The staggering stress of organ transplant protocol forms the dramatic core of organ transplant narration and may be briefly outlined (using heart transplant protocol as a model).

First it must be proved that a patient has less than six months to live without a vital organ transplant. To patients, the news that they are "terminal" may come as a complete surprise. Mary Gohlke, the first successful heart-lung transplant recipient, recounts her shock in her autobiography, *I'll Take Tomorrow*, when she is told she is dying and that there is no cure: "I could scarcely breathe for a moment. I suddenly felt removed from that office. It was as if I saw myself from a distance sitting there as part of the scene. I am sure Dr. Slater could detect no reaction. I was numb inside and out" (20).

Even terminally ill patients may deny their symptoms until they are told an organ transplant is their only option. A. C. Greene, accordingly, describes the day when he is told he must have a heart transplant: "A day of inevitable disability was reached, a day when even hopeless hope had to be suspended. No more pretense of recovery, no more gestures and attempts to cover up what was so obviously a panting, desperate cripple" (46).

Patients soon learn, however, that needing an organ transplant is no guarantee of getting it. In one recent study, only 49% of patients needing heart transplants were accepted as candidates (Siegel, abstract). Due to lack of organ donors, over half of the patients accepted for heart transplants will die before receiving an organ. If donors are available for only one out of four patients, candidates must be chosen selectively. Accordingly, a patient needing a transplant is rigorously screened. Medically, the patient should be relatively young and healthy apart from the disease. Illnesses such as diabetes, kidney disease, pulmonary hypertension, systemic infections, or ongoing substance abuse, may eliminate a patient from consideration (Achuff 52).

The patient must also be screened for psychosocial fitness. Psychosocial tests range from assessments of intelligence or signs of substance abuse in some centers to determining a patient's medical compliance in others (Michalisko 59). In short, transplant teams look for—in Michel Foucault's sense of the term—the most medically and psychologically docile body, the body least likely to physically reject the organ, and most likely to obey the life-long program of treatment and surveillance that will follow. Statistically, for whatever set of reasons, this screening has had very normative results; the average transplant patient—in fact, over three-fourths of all heart transplant patients—winds up being a white, married, heterosexual male, with a mean age of forty-four years (e.g., "Psychiatric Distress" Kuhn 26).

For the patient selected as a heart transplant candidate, the next stage is by far the most stressful. A donor must be found. Further, the donor's body must be screened just as rigorously as the host's. Candidates may only receive the next available organ if they are considered high priority. This, of course, is double jeopardy. By the time patients are ill enough to head a waiting list, they may also die before receiving an organ. Not surprisingly, as many prospective organ-transplant patients get sicker, they actively begin wishing someone would die. One study found that patients and their families begin "wishing for inclement weather because there would be a greater chance for a donor's death. Frierson and Lippmann called this the "'rainy day syndrome,' which is 'often accompanied by significant feelings of guilt'" (Gier 343). Mary Gohlke similarly describes her feelings as she waits for a donor organ: "Intellectually I understood that any transplant depended on someone's death, but I still harbored a little nagging feeling of guilt that I would profit from so tragic an event. I guess I always will" (45).

For the patient reduced to a helpless body—a child—the doctor (whether a man or woman) becomes the father, the site of logos and technology that offers the only means of survival. In organ transplantation, every conceivable variable that may be controlled by technology, *is*. The recipient and donor are screened extensively, and all members of a transplant team are kept abreast of refinements in equipment, medicine, and technique.

In the midst of all this state-of-the-art technology, the donor organ, bearer of life and potential mother, becomes the unknown. No one can completely predict what will happen when the donor organ and body of the host unite. The donor organ may instantly reject and shrivel during surgery or may reject after surgery. Repeated biopsies must be taken to test for rejection; the transplant patient's life becomes one subjected to continual surveillance. Although patients are taught to adjust to the new organ, each biopsy re-awakens all the patients' anxiety, and erodes their ability to deny the body's invasion by a foreign text.

The patient's postoperative adjustment to the organ is seen as an index of health. In one study "pronounced curiosity about the characteristics of donors and their death" was "recorded" but "not rated as *pathologic* ("Psychopathology" Kuhn, emphasis added 27). What, one wonders, in the case of someone providing an organ that allows you to live, would be considered "normal" curiosity? Clearly, patients do struggle as they adjust to their new organ and often practice methods of bonding and separation that mimic one's relationship to his or her original mother. One patient's story parallels Freud's explanation of *fort/da*, the game of disappearance and return Freud uses to show how a child gains mastery of his mother's absence and return. This patient first dreamt his new heart flew out of his body and then, in a later dream, resolved the conflict by a dream in which "he perceived a similarity between the donor and the donor's family and himself and his own family in several important ways" (Allender 230). In short, he accepted the new organ—the new mother—by endowing it with a genealogy—however fictional—that would create a textual graft between the transplanted organ and his body.

Mothering as Metaphor

All the dark, hidden, and uncontrollable aspects of transplantation become displaced onto the transplanted organ. The donor organ becomes a site of ambivalence. It gives life but also, submerged, lies waiting to erupt, a buried "text" that must be continually read but may never be fully understood. The donor organ emerges as the opponent of logos, and becomes the "other." The donor organ, like the mother residing in the conceptual chain leading to disease and death, exceeds our intellectual control and resists order and logic. In *Heartsounds*, Lear speaks of technology's antipathy to that which cannot be tangibly assessed:

> Technique! Land of technology. Doctors of technology. Give them the abnormal heartbeat, the stricture, the germ, the tumor, things they can hear, see, palpate, capture on camera and tape . . . . Whatever cannot be diagnosed or treated by technique is suspect, vaguely inauthentic, and quite possibly does not exist. (216)

The donor organ, however carefully screened and scrutinized by science and technology, remains essentially fickle and unpredictable.

In the patient's reformulated family dynamics following organ transplantation, the roles of mother, father, and child have all been altered. When the positions of father, child, and mother are transposed onto the triad of technology, patient, and donor organ, respectively, the mother's relation to disease is clear. Though the transplanted organ, symbolically operating as mother, gives life, the organ/mother, by rejecting its host, may also give disease and death. While the organ's role may seem more like that of a baby in a womb than that of mother, the donor organ's potential to affect the host's life and death suggests greater (metaphorical) power. Indeed, the organ's placement into the body of the transplant recipient, by a kind of reverse Caesarean section (the "baby" is inserted rather than removed), initiates what could be termed a "hostile takeover." Transplant patients may resist being overcome by the donor organs' antibodies only by shutting down their own immune system. Medically, the patient must become "defenseless," miming the vulnerability of a child, in order to accept the organ. From this standpoint, the donor organ and host operate as mother to child, since, in effect, the organ controls the body. Consistent with this dynamic, most transplant patients displace their gratitude onto the doctor and technology (the position of the father) rather than onto the donor organ, which may, after all, eventually kill them.

Transplantation, then, highlights the metaphoricity of family roles. Postoperatively, the patient symbiotically bonds with other transplant patients. A. C. Greene describes himself and the other transplant patients as a "unique tribe" who remain in "fellowship" because of the "bond of this shared, highly dramatic experience" (147, 148). These patients track each other's progress like closely connected brothers and sisters, and they all suffer when one experiences organ rejection and/or dies. Born of the same father (technology) and mother (body, i.e., the donor organ), the fate of one transplant patient becomes predictive for all.

The mother's relation to body and disease also ensures her erasure. Just as a person gains autonomy by breaking away from his real mother, a transplant patient is encouraged to forget that the transplanted organ came from another body. Successful patients learn to deny any sense of abnormality about their situation and to achieve "psychologic incorporation" of the donor organs by thinking about them as their own ("Psychiatric Distress," Kuhn 27).

Paradoxically, then, culture corrects and effaces the body at the same time. Jean-François Lyotard posits that the ultimate aim of all technology is to create a man not weighed down by body, "to make thinking materially possible" after the body has been destroyed (77). Valie Export, discussing Freud's *Civilization and Its Discontents*, makes the same point: "Technology as the sum of all tools serves thus not only the cultural transformation of nature, but also has the tendency to transform and dissolve the body itself, precisely inasmuch as technology is cultural activity" (2).

Or, even more succinctly—and here we see the enemy isolated—Andreas Huyssen sees the "ultimate technological fantasy" as "creation without the mother" (qtd. in Doane 168). Culture thus poises itself in opposition to body, particularly a woman's messy maternal body, with its "breasts and belly, milk and childbearing" (Export 5).

Though the law of the father has been termed the reality principle, it is also the principle of delusion. For what we learn in entering the symbolic order, the world of culture and technology, is to deny the body. Organ transplantation, like most of technology, works to transcend the body's normal limitations. Yet, the procedure still hinges on the unpredictable organ, the mother, that promises, variously, the options of life, death, and/or disease. The donor organ, synecdochical for both body and mother, bears the blame. When a transplant patient dies, technology is not at fault; *the organ failed.*

For autobiography, key issues of selfhood surface in the tangled psychodynamics of organ transplantation. As bodies fragment and enter or receive parts of other bodies, what happens to the body's boundaries? How does this affect the autobiographer's "signature"? Even the skeptical Paul de Man sees autobiography as an attempt at self-restoration. What self gets restored in the intersection of organ transplantation?

How, too, will gender be inflected by organ transplantation? As Mary Ann Doane speculates, when the "other invades the most private space—the inside of the body—the foundations of subjectivity are shaken" (170). Would a woman who has experienced an analogous "invasion" through the course of pregnancy feel less violated than a man? Do women, having dealt with bodily surveillance to some degree all their lives—e.g., Is my period late? Am I ovulating? Am I pregnant? Am I going through menopause? Is this a lump in my breast?—have less trouble coping with the intensive monitoring transplantation initiates? Will men, like mothers, invaded by another body, and forced to deal intimately with their own bodies, see transplantation as a process of feminization?

These questions, at present, are all unanswerable. Transplantation blurs the margins of subjectivity and ripples the smooth curve from birth to death. Given options, we live and die less innocently. For autobiography, which is always a reflection of how people perceive themselves at given points in history, it is uncertain how the postmodern body—remembered and re-mothered—will write itself. What *is* certain, however, is that our bodies are not the same.

* * * * *

The dynamics of organ transplantation serve to illustrate a central, embedded metaphor in Western culture. Instinctively, a mother is associated with nature, body, birth, death, and the unknown. Men dissociate themselves from the site of motherhood for their own reasons. Perhaps, as Rich speculates, a mother simply evokes too many memories for a man: "He is reminded, somewhere beyond repression, of his existence as a mere speck, a weak, blind clot of flesh growing inside her body" (188). A daughter/woman/mother, however, is haunted by sameness. She knows that in order to be read as mind, she must not be seen as body, particularly as a maternal body.

The re-formulation of family following organ transplantation thus reminds us that family roles are largely cultural and ideological constructions. As Ann Daly remarks, "There have always been mothers, but motherhood was invented" (qtd. in Hirsch 14). Motherhood will remain an invention—a figure systematically erased or minimized in women's autobiographies—as long as motherhood remains unexamined and inadequately theorized.

Gilles Deleuze and Felix Guattari, in their book *Anti-Oedipus: Capitalism and Schizophrenia* also see a liberating impulse in postmodern culture's re-formulation of family roles. Dana Heller, paraphrasing Deleuze and Guattari, explains how the Oedipal model, though useful, oversimplifies the family romance: "Desire is never split along the opposed axes of identification and desire, but is always complexly and simultaneously intertwined with both. The child's identification is never *with* one parent or the other, just as his desire is never *for* one parent or the other" (Heller 36).

Again, summarizing Deleuze and Guattari's argument, Heller states that deconstructing the Oedipal model could be "potentially liberating" by opposing "centeredness, authority, and closed systems, [and] articulating instead an ever-mobile plurality of nonhierarchical desires that are productive and threatening" (37). Quite possibly, the role of the mother might emerge as the "most liberated" figure in the new family romance since traditionally, the Oedipal model has served to silence the mother: "The Freudian family romance constructs the mother as a voiceless and potentially deceptive enclosed space where mysteries of multiple origin are encoded in a language no one can read" (Heller 32).

Because organ transplantation serves to disrupt bodily margins and intersect bodily parts with no regard to gender, these new body technologies also force us to question old concepts. The postmodern body—re-organized and freshly conceived—may be in the process of being rewritten. Writers such as Alta or Nancy Mairs categorically refuse to separate their bodies from their texts. Mairs, as Rich would advocate, writes of her life by "thinking through the body":

> One simply cannot *be* without being a body. One simply *is* inches of supple skin and foot after foot of gut, slosh of blood, thud of heart, lick of tongue, brain humped and folded into skull. And it is as a body that one inhabits the past and it inhabits one's body . . . . Whe-

ther or not I permitted myself to think of my self as a body at some earlier time, I cannot deny the identity today. That identity offers me my only means of entering and literally making sense of my past. ("Bone House" 9)

Mairs' innovative desire to write an autobiography "about" her body, rather than "despite" her body, offers an escape route from the double bind Barbara Johnson describes facing a woman autobiographer: "The problem for the female autobiographer is, on the one hand, to resist the pressure of masculine autobiography as the only literary genre available for her enterprise, and, on the other, to describe a difficulty in conforming to a female ideal which is largely a fantasy of the masculine, not the feminine, imagination" (154). In short, women need to develop new autobiographical models—models that will not encourage them to deny their bodies, their mothers, or their own maternity. That is not to suggest that women begin producing identical autobiographies—all concentrating on their bodies—but that women at least become aware of why they make choices in their life-writing, why they position themselves in a certain way to their bodies and to the site of motherhood.

Women may also have reached the point where they can "play" with their subjectivity and access many of the perverse pleasures formerly accorded only to males who wrote autobiographies. Nancy Mairs, in *Remembering the Bone House*, makes several candid admissions and confessions that do nothing to enhance her image. Her perverse pleasure in confessing, however, demonstrates her willingness and confidence to speak from a position of power. The confessor, who admits her sins, is more honest and thus more powerful than the hypocritical reader (the "*hypocrite lecteur*") who does not. Michel Foucault, speaking specifically about sexual revelation, credits our inclination to confess stemming from perversity: "Modern society is perverse, not in spite of its puritanism or as if from a backlash provoked by its hypocrisy; it is in actual fact, and directly, perverse" ("History" 47). Confession, then, operates like a game of power allowing the confessor the freedom to select what she "brings to light" or to also "evade this power, flee from it, or travesty it" ("History" 45). Mairs demonstrates pleasure in transgressing taboos, in confession's verbal flashdance that thrives on "showing off, scandalizing, or resisting" ("History" 45). Whether one "likes" Mairs' confessions or not, her inclination to reveal her sexuality, her extra-marital affairs, and her non-traditional relationship with her husband, illustrates a woman comfortable enough to take risks.

Structurally, women are also breaking with tradition. Nathalie Sarraute's autobiographical "voices," Alta's disjointed narrative, Dillard's poetic pockets of "time" in many of her autobiographical works (*Holy the Firm*, *A Pilgrim at Tinker's Creek*, or *An American Childhood*) also demonstrate a postmodern impulse. Working against the linear sequence of traditional life stories, women are presenting their lives as a collection of fragments and discontinuities. Like Barthes, in his autobiography *Barthes by Barthes* where he arranges the fragments of his life in alphabetical order, women are deliberately subverting the artifice of presenting life as a continuous flow. In both structure and content, women are "shaking up" the autobiographical traditions that formerly ensured their erasure. Whether women will now feel freer to write from the mother's position, and, correspondingly, to re-read and thus "see" the mother's position in texts where it has often been obscured, remains to be seen.

An interesting study, "Reading 'Snow White': The Mother's Story," by Shuli Barzilai advocates just this type of re-visioning. Barzilai takes the story of "Snow White" and considers the mother's (or, in this case, the stepmother's) perspective. Like so many of the autobiographies discussed in this book, "Snow White" focuses on the daughter's story. In re-casting the story from the mother's perspective, Barzilai provides a provocative interpretation. Instead of a story primarily about a mistreated daughter, "Snow White" becomes the tale "of two women . . . a mother who cannot grow up and a daughter who must" (272). From the mother's perspective "the wish [to remain beautiful] that she has held most dear has turned into a tale of loss and fragmentation" (272). From the daughter's perspective "mother always smothers" and Snow White would like "nothing better than to get this interfering older woman, this deadly dragon-mother, out of her life" (272). Barzilai ends her analysis with an ironic warning: "Yet once more from the mother's perspective: Snow White is going to be ever so sorry when the babies start coming, and the king goes out hunting, and no woman really close and caring is around to help her" (272). In Barzilai's reading the evil mother may have been vanquished, but Snow White's "turn" is coming. To resurrect the mother's role, then, women not only have to be free to write as a mother but be able to *read* as a mother as well.

When I stored each chapter of this book in my computer, the file names formed a loose trajectory of their own. The chapters were stored, respectively, under the words "daughter," "mind," "erotic," "bloody," and "mombody." Similarly, my line of inquiry traveled from daughter to mother, and from mind to body. The first three chapters largely discussed the daughters' point-of-view while the last two chapters considered the mothers' perspective. A corresponding shift was made from autobiographies that highlighted the mind to autobiographies that foregrounded the body. Despite the relative dichotomy this organization suggests, women, as Rich posits, are always both daughters and mothers (whether they actually bear children or not) and are, of course, always a blend of mind and body.

I found when I first began reading women's autobiographies that these works were textually lopsided; women's life-writing has been mostly written *by* daughters about *their* minds. Writers such as Simone de Beauvoir, Nathalie Sarraute, Carol Ascher, Shirley Abbott, Annie Dillard, or Maya Angelou to name a few, focus more on their mother's body than on their mother's mind. Women who have written from the mother's position, like Erma Bombeck, Shirley Jackson, Jean Kerr, or— to a lesser degree—Kathryn Grody used irony to distance themselves from their own positions as mothers. Maxine Hong Kingston and Charlotte Perkins Gilman envisioned motherhood as successful only within the context of fantasy. Though a great deal of feminist theory concentrates on motherhood, it often emerges from the daughter's perspective and uses the mother's body. Similarly, the concepts embedded in Western culture and postmodern technology stand at odds with the embodied, mortally threatening site of motherhood.

Less frequently and more recently, women such as Nancy Mairs, Jane Lazarre, Alta, Ann Roiphe, or Elizabeth Fox-Genovese have begun to write candidly from the mother's position and/or consider the mother's perspective.   Certainly, before productive theorizations can be made about male/female difference in autobiography, the "blind spot" in women's life-writing, i.e., a woman's relationship to her body, to her mother and to motherhood, needs to be confronted. In most instances, however, women autobiographers have avoided rather than confronted, the corporeal and maternal.

In "The Hysterical Male," Arthur and Marilouise Kroker explain how the nineteenth-century clitoris was socially/culturally/medically constructed as a "failed Freudian penis" (xi). In a similar manner, the pervasive view of mother as a "failed" (less active, less intellectual) woman also needs to be recognized for the cultural construction that it is.

Stunted by generic constraints and the intellectual/spiritual course of autobiography, a woman—and particularly a mother—as an autobiographical subject is often doomed to become instead an object, *subjected*. Culturally, theoretically, and autobiographically, motherhood remains an uneasy site: best ignored than explored.   Conversely, this book has probed the mechanics of subjection, the resonant textual silences that fail to repress the body and the mother in women's autobiography, culture, and feminism.

Bibliography

Abbot, Shirley. "Excerpt from *Womenfolks: Growing Up Down South.*" *Mothers: Memories, Dreams and Reflections by Literary Daughters.* Ed. Susan Cahill. New York and Scarborough, Ontario: New American Library, 1988. 1–24.

Achuff, Stephen C., M.D., et al. "Potential Contraindications to Cardiac Transplantation." *Heart and Heart Lung Transplantation.* Eds. William A. Bargarther, M.D., Bruce A. Reitz, M.D., and Stephen Achuff. Philadelphia: Saunders, 1990. 54–56.

Adams, Henry. *The Education of Henry Adams.* Boston: Houghton Mifflin, 1961.

Allender, James, M.D., et al. "Stages of Psychological Adjustment with Heart Transplantation." *Journal of Heart Transplantation.* 2:3 (1983): 228–31.

Allfrey, Phyllis Shand. "Phyllis Shand Allfrey *talking* with Polly Pattullo. *Writing Lives: Conversations between Women Writers.* Ed. Mary Chamberlain. London: Virago Press, 1988. 224–234.

Alta. *Momma: a start on all the untold stories.* New York: Times Change Press, 1974.

Angelou, Maya. *I Know Why the Caged Bird Sings.* New York: Bantam, 1969.

————. "Maya Angelou *talking* with Rosa Guy." *Writing Lives: Conversations Between Women Writers.* Ed. Mary Chamberlain. London: Virago Press, 1988. 1-14.

Ascher, Carol. "Remembering Berlin—1979." *My Mother's Daughter: Stories by Women.* Ed. Irene Zahava. Freedom: The Crossing Press, 1991. 172–188.

Auerbach, Eric. *Mimesis: The Representation of Reality in Western Literature.* Princeton: Princeton University Press, 1953.

Bair, Deirdre. *Simone de Beauvoir: A Biography.* New York: Summit Books, 1990.

Barthes, Roland. *Mythologies*. New York: Hill and Wang, 1957.

————. *The Pleasure of the Text*. New York: Hill and Wang, 1975.

————. *Roland Barthes by Roland Barthes*. New York: Hill and Wang, 1977.

Barzilai, Shuli. "Reading *Snow White*: The Mother's Story." *Ties That Bind: Essays on Mothering and Patriarchy*. Eds. Jean F. O' Barr, Deborah Pope, and Mary Wyer. Chicago and London: University of Chicago Press, 1990.

Bataille, Georges. *Eroticism: Death and Sensuality*. San Francisco: City Lights Books, 1986.

Baudrillard, Jean. *Seduction*. New York: St. Martin's Press, 1979.

Beauvoir, Simone de. *Memoirs of a Dutiful Daughter*. New York: Harper and Row, 1958.

————. *The Second Sex*. New York: Knopf, 1971.

————. *A Very Easy Death*. New York: Putnam's, 1964.

Benjamin, Jessica. *The Bonds of Love*. New York: Pantheon, 1988.

Benstock, Shari, ed. *The Private Self: Theory and Practice of Women's Autobiographical Writings*. Chapel Hill and London: University of North Carolina Press, 1988.

Bergland, Martha. *A Farm Under a Lake*. New York: Vintage Books, 1989.

Binchy, Maeve. Untitled essay. *A Portrait of the Artist as a Young Girl*. Ed. John Quinn. London: Methuen, 1986. 3–15.

Blau, Herbert. *The Eye of Prey: Subversions of the Postmodern*. Bloomington and Indianapolis: Indiana University Press, 1987.

Bloom, Lynn Z., and Orlee Holder. "Anais Nin's *Diary* in Context." *Women's Autobiography:Essays in Criticism*. Ed. Estelle Jelinek. Boston: Twayne, 1986. 206–20.

————. "Promises Fulfilled: Positive Images of Women in Twentieth Century Autobiography." *Feminist Criticism: Theory, Poetry and Prose*. Eds. Cheryl L. Brown and Karen Olson, Metuchen, NJ, and London: Scarecrow Press, 1978. 324–38.

Bloomingdale, Teresa. *Sense and Momsense*. Garden City, NY: Doubleday, 1986.

Bombeck, Erma. *Family: The Ties That Bind and Gag*. New York: McGraw-Hill, 1987.

——. *The Grass Is Always Greener Over the Septic Tank*. Greenwich: Fawcett Publications, 1976.

——. *Just Wait Till You Have Children of Your Own*. Garden City and New York: Doubleday, 1971.

——. *Motherhood: The Second Oldest Profession*. New York: McGraw-Hill, 1983.

Bordo, Susan. "Reading the Slender Body." *Body/Politics: Women and the Discourses of Science*. Eds. Mary Jacobus, Evelyn Fox Keller, and Sally Shuttleworth. New York: Routledge, 1990. 83–112.

Boulos-Walker, Michelle. *Philosophy and the Maternal Body: Reading Silence*. London and New York: Routledge, 1998.

Bowen, Elizabeth. "Excerpt from *Memories of a Dublin Childhood*." *Mothers: Memories, Dreams and Reflections by Literary Daughters*. Ed. Susan Cahill. New York and Scarborough: New American Library, 1988. 39–47.

Bradbury Malcolm and James McFarlene, eds. *Modernism*. Harmondsworth: Penguin, , 1986.

Briscoe, Mary Louise, ed. *American Autobiography: 1945–1980: A Bibliography*. Madison: University of Wisconsin Press, 1982.

Brodski, Bella, and Celeste Schenck, eds. *Life/Lines: Theorizing Women's Autobiography*. Ithaca and London: Cornell University Press, 1988.

Brooks, Peter. *Reading for the Plot: Design and Intention in Narrative*. New York: Vintage Books, 1984.

Bucior, Carolyn. "A Day of Death, Years of Living." *Wisconsin Magazine* 21 Oct. 1990: 6–16.

Cahill, Susan, ed. *Mothers: Memories, Dreams and Reflections by Literary Daughters*. New York and Scarborough, Ontario: New American Library, 1988.

Chernin, Kim. *In My Mother's House: A Daughter's Story*. New York: Harper, 1983.

Chodorow, Nancy. *The Reproduction of Mothering: Psychoanalysis and the Sociology of Gender*. Berkeley: University of California Press, 1978.

Christian, Barbara, ed. *Black Feminist Criticism: Perspectives on Black Women Writers*. Oxford and London: Pergamon Press, 1985.

Cixous, Hélène. "The Laugh of the Medusa." *Critical Theory Since 1965*. Ed. Hazard Adams and Leroy Searles. Tallahassee: Florida State University Press, 1986. 309–21.

————. "Sorties: Out & Out: Attacks/Ways Out/Forays." *Contemporary Critical Theory*. Ed. Dan Latimer. San Diego: Harcourt. 1989. 558–78.

Clifford, Gay. *The Transformations of Allegory From Spenser to Hawthorne*. London and Boston: Routledge, 1974.

Corbin, Laurie. *The Mother Mirror: Self-Representation and the Mother-Daughter Relation in Colette, Simone de Beauvoir, and Marguerite Duras*. New York: Peter Lang Publishing, 1996.

Cudjoe, Selwyn. "Maya Angelou and the Autobiographical Statement." *Black Feminist Criticism: Perspectives on Black Women Writers*. Barbara Christian. Oxford and London: Pergamon Press, 1989. 185–99.

Cunningham, F. Gary, et al. *Williams Obstetrics*. 19th ed. Norwalk: Appleton & Lange, 1993.

Davison, Jaquie. *I Am a Housewife!* New York: Guild Books, 1972.

Dayus, Kathleen. "Kathleen Dayus *talking* with Mary Chamberlain." *Writing Lives: Conversations between Women Writers*. Ed. Mary Chamberlain. London: Virago Press, 1988, 57–67.

Deleuze, Gilles, and Felix Guattari. *Anti-Oedipus: Capitalism and Schizophrenia*. Trans. Robert Hurley, Mark Seem, and Helen R. Lane. Minneapolis: University of Minnesota Press, 1983.

de Man, Paul. "Autobiography as De-Facement." *MLN* 94 (1979): 919–30.

—————. *Allegories of Reading: Figural Language in Rousseau, Nietzsche, Rilke, and Proust.* New Haven: Yale University Press, 1979.

—————. *Blindness and Insight: Essays in the Rhetoric of Contemporary Criticism.* New York: Oxford University Press, 1971.

Derrida, Jacques. *The Ear of the Other: Otobiography, Transference, Translation.* Lincoln and London: University of Nebraska Press, 1985.

Devlin, Polly. Untitled essay. *A Portrait of an Artist as a Young Girl.* Ed. John Quinn. London: Methuen, 1986. 33–48.

Dillard, Annie. *An American Childhood.* New York: Harper and Row, 1987.

—————. *Holy the Firm.* New York: Harper and Row, 1977.

—————. *Pilgrim at Tinker Creek.* New York: Harper's Magazine Press, 1974.

Dinnerstein, Dorothy. *The Mermaid and the Minotaur.* New York: Harper, 1976.

Doane, Mary Ann. "Technophilia: Technology, Representation, and the Feminine." *Body/Politics: Women and the Discourses of Science.* Eds. Mary Jacobus, Evelyn FoxKeller, and Sally Shuttleworth. New York: Routledge, 1990. 163–76.

Du Maurier, Daphne. *Myself When Young: The Shaping of a Writer.* New York: Doubleday and Company, 1977.

Eakin, Paul John. *Fictions in Autobiography: Studies in the Art of Self-Invention.* Princeton: Princeton University Press, 1985.

Eastman, Nicholson J., ed. *Williams Obstetrics.* 10th ed. New York: Appleton-Century-Crofts, 1950.

Edwards, Susan. *Erma Bombeck: A Life in Humor.* New York: Avon Books, 1997.

Eisenstein, Hester, and Alice Jardine, eds. *The Future of Difference.* Boston: G.K. Hall and Company, 1980.

Evans, Mary. "Views of Women and Men in the Work of Simone de
    Beauvoir." *Critical Essays on Simone de Beauvoir.* Ed. Elaine
    Marks. Boston: G. K. Hall and Company, 1987. 172–83.

Export, Valie. "The Real and Its Double: The Body." *Center for Twenti-
    eth Century Studies.* University of Wisconsin-Milwaukee, Working
    Paper no. 7, Fall 1988.

Flax, Jane. "Mother-Daughter Relationships: Psychodynamics, Politics,
    and Philosophy." *The Future of Difference.* Eds. Hester Eisenstein
    and Alice Jardine, Boston: G. K. Hall & Co., 1980. 20–40.

————. *Thinking Fragments: Psychoanalysis, Feminism and Post-
    modernism in the Contemporary West.* Berkeley: University of
    California Press, 1990.

Fletcher, Angus. *Allegory: The Theory of a Symbolic Mode.* Ithaca and
    London: Cornell University Press, 1964.

Foucault, Michel. *Discipline and Punish: The Birth of the Prison.*
    Trans. Alan Sheridan. New York: Vintage Books, 1979.

————. "Of Other Spaces." *Diacritics* 16.1 (1986): 22–27.

Fox-Genovese, Elizabeth. *"Feminism Is Not the Story of My Life"*: *How
    Today's Feminist Elite Has Lost Touch with the Real Concerns of
    Women.* New York: Anchor Books, 1996.

Friedan, Betty. *The Feminine Mystique.* New York: Norton, 1961.

French, Marilyn. *The Women's Room.* New York: Harcourt, 1977.

Freud, Sigmund. *Civilization and Its Discontents.* New York and Lon-
    don: Norton, 1961.

Friday, Nancy. *My Mother/My Self.* New York: Delacorte Press, 1977.

Frye, Northrop. *Anatomy of Criticism: Four Essays.* Princeton: Prince-
    ton University Press, 1957.

Gallop, Jane. *The Daughter's Seduction: Feminism and Psychoanalysis.*
    Ithaca, NY: Cornell University Press, 1982.

Gardiner, Judith Kegan. "On Female Identity and Writing About
    Women." *Writing and Sexual Differences.* Ed. Elizabeth Abel.
    Chicago: University of Chicago Press, 1982. 177–92.

Garner, Shirley Nelson, Claire Kuhane, and Madelon Sprengnether, eds. *The (M)other Tongue: Essays in Feminist Psychoanalytic Interpretation.* Ithaca and London: Cornell University Press, 1985.

Gier, Martha, et al. "Stress Reduction with Heart Transplant Patients and Their Families: A Multidisciplinary Approach." *Journal of Heart Transplantation.* 7:5 (1982): 342–47.

Gilchrist, Ellen. *Falling Through Space.* Boston: Little and Brown, 1987.

Gilligan, Carol. *In a Different Voice: Psychological Theory and Women's Development.* Cambridge: Harvard University Press, 1982.

Gilman, Charlotte Perkins. *Herland.* New York: Pantheon, 1979.

————. *The Living of Charlotte Perkins Gilman.* New York: Harper, 1935.

————. *Moving the Mountain.* New York: Charlton Co. 1911.

————. *With Her in Ourland.* Serialized in *The Forerunner.* (1916).

————. *The Yellow Wallpaper.* New York: Feminist Press, 1973.

Gilmore, Leigh. *Autobiographics: A Feminist Theory of Women's Self-Representation.* Ithaca and London: Cornell University Press, 1994.

Glasgow, Ellen. *The Woman Within.* New York: Harcourt, 1954.

Gohlke, Mary, with Max Jennings. *I'll Take Tomorrow.* New York: Evans & Co., 1985.

Goodman, Ellen. *Close to Home.* New York: Simon, 1979.

Gornick, Vivian. *Fierce Attachments: A Memoir.* New York: Touchstone, 1987.

Greene, A. C. *Taking Heart.* New York: Simon, 1990.

Grody, Kathryn. *A Mom's Life.* New York: Avon, 1991.

Gusdorf, Georges. "Conditions and Limits of Autobiography." *Autobiography: Essays Theoretical and Critical.* Ed. James Olney. Princeton: Princeton University Press, 1980. 28–48.

Gutkind, Lee. *Many Sleepless Nights.* New York: Norton, 1988.

Hancock, Emily. *The Girl Within.* New York: Fawcett Columbine, 1989.

Hassan, Ihab. *Out of Egypt: Scenes and Arguments of an Autobiography*. Carbondale and Edwardsville: Southern Illinois University Press, 1986.

————. *The Postmodern Turn: Essays in Postmodern Theory and Culture*. Columbus: Ohio State University Press, 1987.

Hazo, Samuel. Review of *An American Childhood* by Annie Dillard. *Commonweal* 6 Nov.1987: 636.

Heilbrun, Carolyn G. *Writing a Woman's Life*. New York: Ballantine Books, 1988.

Heller, Dana. *Family Plots: The De-Oedipalization of Popular Culture*. Philadelphia: University of Pennsylvania Press, 1995.

Hewitt, Leah. *Autobiographical Tightropes*. Lincoln and London: University of Nebraska Press, 1990.

Hirsch, Marianne. *The Mother/Daughter Plot: Narrative, Psychoanalysis, Feminism*. Bloomington and Indianapolis: Indiana University Press, 1989.

Hoffman, Eva. *Lost in Translation: A Life in a New Language*. New York: Penguin Books, 1989.

Hurston, Zora Neale. *Dust Tracks on a Road*. [1942]. Urbana and Chicago: University of Chicago Press, 1984.

Irigaray, Luce. "And the One Doesn't Stir Without the Other." Trans. Helene Vivian Wenzel. *Signs: Journal of Women in Culture and Society* 7.1 (1981): 60–67.

————. *This Sex Which Is Not One*. Ithaca, NY: Cornell University Press, 1985.

Jackson, Shirley. *Life among the Savages*. Chicago: Academy Chicago Publishers, 1990.

————. "The Renegade" *The Magic of Shirley Jackson*. Ed. Stanley Edgar Hyman. New York: Farrar, 1966. 40–51.

————. "The Tooth." Hyman, 120–36.

————. *Raising Demons*. Hyman, 531–753.Jardine, Alice. "Death Sentences: Writing Couples and Ideology." *The Female Body in*

Western Culture. Ed. Susan Rubin Suleiman. Cambridge: Harvard University Press, 1986. 84–98.

————. *Gynesis: Configurations of Woman and Modernity*. Ithaca: Cornell University Press, 1985.

Jay, Gregory. *America the Scrivener: Deconstruction and the Subject of Literary History*. Ithaca and London: Cornell University Press, 1990.

Jelinek, Estelle. "Discontinuity and Order: A Comparison of Women's and Men's Autobiographies." Division on Feminist Biography and Autobiography, MLA Convention, New York, 1976.

————. *The Tradition of Women's Autobiography from Antiquity to the Present*. Boston: Twayne, 1986.

————. *Women's Autobiography: Essays in Criticism*. Bloomington: Indiana University Press, 1980.

Johnson, Barbara. *A World of Difference*. Baltimore and London: Johns Hopkins University Press, 1987.

Jones, Ann Rosalind. "Writing the Body: Toward an Understanding of *L'Ecriture Féminine*." *Feminist Studies* 7.2 (Summer 1981): 247–63.

Joyrich, Lynne. "Television and the Cyborg Subject(ed)." *Center for Twentieth Century Studies*. University of Wisconsin-Milwaukee. Working Paper no. 8 (Fall/Winter 1989–1990).

Juhasz, Suzanne. "Some Deep Old Desk or Capacious Hold-All: Form and Women's Autobiography." *College English* 39 (1978): 663–68.

————. "Towards a Theory of Form in Feminist Autobiography: Kate Millet's *Flying* and *Sita*; Maxine Hong Kingston's *The Woman Warrior*." *Women's Autobiography: Essays in Criticism*. Ed. Estelle Jelinek. Bloomington: Indiana University Press. 221–37.

Kaplan, Ann E. "Is the Gaze Male?" *Powers of Desire: The Politics of Sexuality*. Eds. Ann Snitow, Christine Stansell, and Sharon Thompson. New York: Monthly Review Press, 1983.

Kerr, Jean. *How I Got to Be Perfect*. Garden City: Doubleday, 1978.

————. *Please Don't Eat the Daisies*. Garden City: Doubleday, 1954.

King, Florence. *Confessions of a Failed Southern Lady*. New York: St. Martin's Press, 1985.

Kingston, Maxine Hong. *The Woman Warrior: Memories of a Girlhood Among Ghosts*. New York: Vintage Books, 1975.

Kloepfer, Deborah Kelly. *The Unspeakable Mother: Forbidden Discourse in Jean Rhys and H. D.* Ithaca and London: Cornell University Press, 1989.

Kristeva, Julia. "About Chinese Women." *The Kristeva Reader*. Ed. Toril Moi. New York: Columbia University Press, 1986. 138–59.

————. "Stabat Mater." *The Female Body in Western Culture: Comptemporary Perspectives*. Ed. Susan Rubin Suleiman. Cambridge and London: Harvard University Press. 99–118.

Kroker, Arthur, and Marilouise Kroker. "The Hysterical Male: One Libido?" *The Hysterical Male: New Feminist Theory*. Eds. Arthur Kroker and Marilouise Kroker. New York: St. Martin's Press, 1991. ix–xiv.

Kuczkir, Mary. *My Dishtowel Flies at Half-Mast*. New York: Ballantine, 1980.

Kuhane, Claire. "The Gothic Mirror." *The (M)other Tongue: Essays in Feminist Psychoanalytic Interpretation*. Eds. Shirley Nelson Garner, Claire Kuhane, and Madelon Sprengnether. Ithaca and London: Cornell University Press. 334–51.

Kuhn, Wolfgang F. "Psychiatric Distress During Stages of the Heart Protocol." *Journal of Heart Transplantation* 9.1 (1990): 25–29.

————. "Psychopathology in Heart Transplant Patients." *Journal of Heart Transplantation* 7:3 (1988):223–26.

Lane, Ann J. *To Herland and Beyond: The Life and Work of Charlotte Perkins Gilman*. New York: Pantheon Books, 1990.

Latimer, Dan, ed. *Contemporary Critical Theory*. San Diego: Harcourt, 1989.

Lavin, Mary. Untitled essay. *A Portrait of the Artist as a Young Girl.* Ed. John Quinn. London: Methuen, 1986. 79–92.

Lazarre, Jane. *The Mother Knot.* New York: McGraw-Hill, 1976.

Lear, Martha Weinman. *Heartsounds.* New York: Pocket Books, 1980.

Lehmann, Rosamond. "Rosamond Lehmann *talking* with Janet Watts." *Writing Lives: Conversations between Women Writers.* Ed. Mary Chamberlain. London: Virago Press, 1988, pp. 147–160.

Leiris, Michel. *Manhood: A Journey From Childhood Into the Fierce Order of Virility.* New York: Grossman Publishers, 1963.

Lorde, Audre. *Zami: A New Spelling of My Name.* New York: The Crossing Press, 1983.

Lyotard, Jean-François. "Can Thought Go On Without a Body?" *Discourse* 11.1 (1988–89): 74–87.

MacDonald, Betty. *The Egg and I.* Philadelphia: Lippincott Company, 1945.

————. *Onions in the Stew.* Philadelphia and New York: Lippincott, 1954.

Mairs, Nancy. *Ordinary Time: Cycles in Marriage, Faith, and Renewal.* Boston: Beacon Press, 1993.

————. *Plaintext.* New York: Harper & Row, 1986.

————. *Remembering the Bone House: An Erotics of Space and Place.* Grand Rapids: Harper, 1989.

Marks, Elaine, ed. *Critical Essays on Simone de Beauvoir.* Boston: G. K. Hall & Co., 1987.

Martineau, Harriet. *Harriett Martineau's Autobiography.* Vol. I. Boston: James R. Osgood & Co., 1877.

Mason, Mary G. "The Other Voice: Autobiographies of Women Writers." *Autobiography: Essays Theoretical and Critical.* Ed. James Olney. Princeton: Princeton University Press, 1980.

McCarthy, Mary. *How I Grew.* San Diego: Harcourt, 1987.

————. *Memories of a Catholic Girlhood.* San Diego: Harcourt, 1957.

McKay, Nellie Y. "Race, Gender, and Cultural Context in Zora Neale Hurston's *Dust Tracks on a Road.*" *Life/Lines: Theorizing Women's Autobiography.* Ed. Bella Brodski and Celeste Schenck. Ithaca and London: Cornell University Press, 1988. 175–88.

Michalisko, Helen O., M. S. W. "Psychosocial Aspects of Recipients Undergoing Heart Transplant." *Heart and Heart-Lung Transplantation.* Eds. William A. Baumgartner, M.S., Bruce Reitz, M.D., and Stephen Achuff. Philadelphia: Saunders, 1990: 54–56.

Miller, J. Hillis. "Theory and Practice: Response to Vincent Leitch [Essay entitled: " The Lateral Dance: The Deconstructive Criticism of J. Hillis Miller]." *Critical Inquiry 6* (1980): 593–607.

Miller, Nancy K. *The Poetics of Gender: Feminist Literary Theory.* New York: Columbia University Press, 1986.

Moffatt, Mary Jane. "Giving My Mother a Bath." *My Mother's Daughter: Stories by Women.* Ed. Irene Zahava, Freedom, California: The Crossing Press, 1991. 92–103.

Moi, Toril. *Simone de Beauvoir: The Making of an Intellectual Woman.* Oxford, UK ; Cambridge, USA : Blackwell, 1994.

Morgan, Janice, and Colette T. Hall. *Redefining Autobiography in Twentieth-Century Women's Fiction: An Essay Collection.* New York: Garland Publishing, 1991.

Munro, Eleanor. *Memoirs of a Modernist Daughter.* New York: Penguin Books, 1988.

Murphy, Delva. "Delva Murphy." *Portrait of the Artist as a Young Girl.* Ed. John Quinn. London: Methuen, 1986. 111–31.

Nabokov, Vladimir. *Speak, Memory: An Autobiography Revisited.* New York: Capricorn Books, 1960.

Neuman, Shirley. "Autobiography and the Construction of the Feminine Body." *Signature* 2 (Winter 1989): 1–26.

O'Callaghan, Raylene. "Voice(s) in Sarraute's *Enfance.*" *New Zealand Journal of French Studies* 9.1 (1988): 83–94.

Olsen, Tillie. *Mother to Daughter Daughter to Mother.* Old Westbury, NY: The Feminist Press, 1984.

Patterson, Yolanda. *Simone de Beauvoir and the Demystification of Motherhood.* Ann Arbor: UMI Research Press, 1989.

Perrin, Noel. "Her Inexhaustible Mind." Review of *An American Childhood* by Annie Dillard. *New York Times Book Review* 27 Sep. 1987: (7).

Piercy, Marge. "Autobiography." *The Cream City Review.* 14.1 (Spring 1990): 3–5.

Ping-Ying, Hsieh. *Autobiography of a Chinese Girl.* Trans. by Tsuichi. London and New York: Pandora, 1986 (1943).

Pritchard, Jack A., Paul C. MacDonald, and Norman F. Gant. *Williams Obstetrics.* 17th ed. Norwalk, CT: Appleton-Century-Crofts, 1985.

Quinn, John, ed. *The Portrait of the Artist as a Young Girl.* London: Methuen, 1986.

Ramsey, Raylene L. *The French New Autobiographies: Sarraute, Duras, and Robbe-Grillet.* Gainesville: University Press of Florida, 1996.

Rich, Adrienne. *Of Woman Born: Motherhood as Experience and Institution.* [Tenth Anniversary Edition] New York: Norton, 1986.

Richardson, Henry Handel. *Myself When Young.* New York: Norton, 1948.

Roiphe, Anne. *Fruitful—Living the Contradictions: A Memoir of Modern Motherhood.* New York: Penquin Books, 1997.

Rousseau, Jean-Jacques. *The Confessions.* Trans. and with an introd. J. M. Cohen. Harmondsworth, Middlesex, England: Penguin Books, 1953.

Roy, Claude. "Simone de Beauvoir." *Critical Essays on Simone de Beauvoir.* Ed. Elaine Marks. Boston: G.K. Hall & Co., 1987. 77–83.

Russ, Joanna. "Recent Feminist Utopias." *Future Females: A Critical Anthology.* Bowling Green: Bowling Green University Popular Press, 1981.

Sarraute, Nathalie. *Childhood.* Trans. Barbara Wright. New York: George Braziller, 1984.

Sartre, Jean-Paul. *The Words*. Trans. Bernard Frechtman. New York: Vintage Books, 1964.

Schwarzer, Alice. *After the Second Sex*. New York: Pantheon Books, 1984.

Siegel, Ronald, M.D., and Robert McManus. "Patients Who Die Awaiting Heart Transplantation." Abstract, *Conference of American College of Cardiology*. Atlanta, March 1991.

Simons, Margaret A., ed. *Feminist Interpretations of Simone de Beauvoir*. University Park: Pennsylvania State University Press, 1995.

Smart, Carol. "Deconstructing Motherhood." *Good Enough Mothering? Perspectives on Lone Motherhood*. Ed. Elizabeth Bortolaia. London: Routledge, 1996.

Smith, Sidonie. *A Poetics of Women's Autobiography: Marginality and the Fictions of Self-Representation*. Bloomington and Indianapolis: Indiana University Press, 1987.

—————. *Subjectivity, Identity, and the Body: Women's Autobiographical Practices in the Twentieth Century*. Bloomington: Indiana University Press, 1993.

Spacks, Patricia. "Reflecting Women." *Yale Review* 63 (1973): 26–42.

—————. "Women's Stories, Women's Selves." *Hudson Review* 30 (1977): 29–46.

Spector, Judith. "Science Fiction and the Sex War: A Womb of One's Own." *Gender Studies: New Directions in Feminist Criticism*. Ed. Judith Spector. Bowling Green: Bowling Green State University Popular Press, 1986.

Stanton, Domna. "Autogynography: Is the Subject Different?" *The Female Autograph*. Eds. Domna Stanton and Jeanine Parsier Plottel. New York: NY Literary Forum, 1984.

—————. "Difference on Trial: A Critique of the Maternal Metaphor in Cixous, Irigaray, and Kristeva." *The Poetics of Gender*. Ed. Nancy K. Miller. New York: Columbia University Press, 1986. 157–82.

Stanton, Elizabeth Cady. *Eighty Years and More*. London: Source Book Press, 1970.

Suleiman, Susan Rubin, ed. *The Female Body in Western Culture: Contemporary Perspectives.* Cambridge and London: Harvard University Press, 1986.

————. "Writing and Motherhood." *The (M)other Tongue: Essays in Feminist Psychoanalytic Interpretation.* Eds. Shirley Nelson Garner, Claire Kuhane, and Madelon Sprengnether. Ithaca and London: Cornell University Press, 1985. 352–77.

Thompson, Thomas. *Hearts: Of Surgeons and Transplants, Miracles and Disasters along the Cardiac Frontier.* New York: McCall Publishing Co., 1971.

Thurer, Shari L. *The Myths of Motherhood: How Culture Reinvents the Good Mother.* New York: Penguin Books, 1994.

Voss, Norrine. "'Saying the Unsayable': An Introduction to Women's Autobiography." *Gender Studies: New Directions in Feminist Criticism.* Ed. Judith Spector. Bowling Green: Bowling Green State University Press, 1986. 218–33.

Walker, Nancy A. *A Very Serious Thing: Women's Humor and American Culture.* Minneapolis: University of Minnesota Press, 1988.

Wallace, Michele. "Variations on Negation and the Heresy of Black Feminist Creativity." *Reading Black, Reading Feminist.* Ed. Henry Louis Gates, Jr., New York: Meridian, 1990.

Watson, Julia, and Sidonie Smith, eds. *De/Colonizing the Subject: The Politics of Gender in Women's Autobiography.* Minneapolis: University of Minnesota Press, 1992.

"Weaning." *thirtysomething.* Written by Liberty Godshall; directed by John Pasquin. Episode no.1.8, December 8, 1987.

Weisman, Mary-Lou. Untitled essay. *Hers: Through Women's Eyes.* Ed. Nancy R. Newhouse. New York: Harper, 1986. 36–39.

Welty, Eudora. "Listening." *Mothers: Memories, Dreams and Reflections by Literary Daughters.* Ed. Susan Cahill. New York and Scarborough: New American Library, 1988, pp. 276-284.

————. *One Writer's Beginnings.* Cambridge and London: Harvard University Press, 1984.

Wenzel, Hélène V., "Interview with Simone de Beauvoir." *Simone de Beauvoir: Witness to a Century.* Ed. Hélène V. Wenzel. *Yale French Studies* 72 (1986): 5-24.

Wharton, Edith. *A Backward Glance.* New York: Scribner's, 1933.

Wilde, Oscar. *The Importance of Being Earnest. Playreader's Repertory: Drama on Stage.* Eds. Melvin R. White and Frank M. Whiting. Glenview, IL: Scott Foresman and Company, 1970. 349–99.

Winston, Elizabeth. "The Autobiographer and Her Readers: From Apology to Affirmation." *Women's Autobiography: Essays in Criticism.* Ed. Estelle Jelinek. Bloomington: Indiana University Press, 1980. 93-111.

Woodward, Kathleen. "Simone de Beauvoir: Aging and Its Discontents." *The Private Self: Theory and Practice of Women's Autobiographical Writings.* Ed. Shari Benstock. Chapel Hill and London: University of North Carolina Press, 1988. 90–113.

————. *Aging and Its Discontents.* Bloomington: Indiana University Press, 1991.

Woolf, Virginia. Excerpt from *Moments of Being. Mothers: Memories, Dreams and Reflections by Literary Daughters.* Ed. Susan Cahill. New York and Scarborough, Ontario: New American Library, 1988. 303–31.

————. *A Room of One's Own.* San Diego: Harcourt, 1929.

Yesierska, Anzia. *Red Ribbon on a White Horse.* Introd. W. H. Auden. New York: Persea Books, 1950.

Zinsser, William, ed. *Inventing the Truth: The Art and Craft of Memoir.* Boston: Houghton Mifflin Company, 1987.

Index